THE CRUCIFIED MESSIAH

THE CRUCIFIED MESSIAH

and other essays

NILS ALSTRUP DAHL

Augsburg Publishing House
Minneapolis, Minnesota

THE CRUCIFIED MESSIAH

Copyright (c) 1974 Augsburg Publishing House

Library of Congress Catalog Card No. 74-14189

International Standard Book No. 0-8066-1469-2

Scripture quotations unless otherwise noted are from the Revised
Standard Version of the Bible, copyright 1946, 1952, and 1971 by
the Division of Christian Education of the National Council of
Churches.

Manufactured in the United States of America

CONTENTS

Preface   7

The Crucified Messiah   10

The Messiahship of Jesus in Paul   37

The Problem of the Historical Jesus   48

Rudolf Bultmann's _Theology of the New Testament_   90

Eschatology and History in Light of the Qumran Texts   129

The Atonement--An Adequate Reward for the Akedah?   146

Postscript   161

Notes   167

ACKNOWLEDGEMENTS

The essays in this volume appeared originally in the following publications:

THE CRUCIFIED MESSIAH was first published in Der historische Jesus und der kerygmatische Christus, ed. by H. Ristow and K. Matthiae, Berlin: Evangelische Verlagsanstalt, 1960.

THE MESSIAHSHIP OF JESUS IN PAUL was originally published in Studia Paulina: in Honorem Johannis de Zwaan, Septuagenarii, ed. by J. N. Sevenster and W. C. van Unnik, Haarlem: De Erven Bohn bv Uitgevers, 1953.

THE PROBLEM OF THE HISTORICAL JESUS is reprinted from Kerygma and History, ed. by Carl E. Braaten and Roy A. Harrisville. Copyright (c) 1962 by Abingdon Press.

RUDOLF BULTMANN'S THEOLOGY OF THE NEW TESTAMENT is translated from Theologische Rundschau 22 (1954) 21-49.

HISTORY AND ESCHATOLOGY IN LIGHT OF THE QUMRAN TEXTS appeared originally in Zeit und Geschichte, Dankesgabe an Rudolf Bultmann zum 80. Geburtstag, ed. by Erich Dinkler, Tübingen: J. C. B. Mohr (Paul Siebeck), 1964.

THE ATONEMENT--AN ADEQUATE REWARD FOR THE AKEDAH? is reprinted from Neotestamentica et Semitica, Studies in Honor of Matthew Black, ed. by Ellis and Wilcox, Edinburgh: T. & T. Clark Ltd., 1969.

PREFACE

The essays in this volume were written over a number of
years. They reflect some aspects of my own biography: Norwegian background and training; early and continuous exposure
to German scholarship; and later a shift to a more pluralistic,
American environment. Among active professors I am in the un-
usual position of being only one generation removed from scholars of the late nineteenth century. My teacher and predecessor
at the University of Oslo, Lyder Brun, was professor from 1897-
1940. A pioneer of biblical criticism in Norway, he was open to
new impulses like form-criticism. But he avoided all extreme
positions and continued in the tradition of careful exegesis
into which he had himself been introduced through commentaries
like those of Bernhard Weiss.

In the early 1930s the Norwegian theological scene was
still dominated by a conflict between conservative and liberal
theology which dated back to the time before World War I. To
a young student, this conflict seemed sterile and obsolete.
Fresh winds were blowing from theological storm-centers on the
continent. Men like Karl Barth and Emil Brunner showed a way
out of the impasse. But we did not buy their theologies whole-
sale. Some of us found that we had to go back to the pioneer-
ing works of the radical German scholars at the turn of the
century, such as Johannes Weiss and Albert Schweitzer, Wrede,
Heitmueller, and Bousset, and certainly Hermann Gunkel and
Julius Wellhausen.

The work of these men made a great impression, mainly
because of the intellectual honesty and rigorous scholarship
which led them to results that undercut the foundations of
European bourgeois religious liberalism which they themselves
represented. Eschatology, worship of Jesus as kyrios, church,

7

sacraments, religious enthusiasm, and even dogma emerged as
genuine elements of New Testament Christianity. From a Norwegian perspective the work of Rudolf Bultmann, like that of
Anton Fridrichsen (who had just moved from Oslo to Uppsala
when I began my studies) was fascinating mainly as an attempt
to come to terms theologically with the findings of the radical critics in the preceding generation.

Later we learned that their historical results were not as
easily converted into neo-orthodoxy as we thought in the 1930s.
But I have retained the conviction that respect for the texts
and the historical realities is the first duty of the New Testament scholar. Throughout my career I have to a great degree,
explicitly or implicitly, been occupied with problems raised
by the pioneers at the beginning of this century. Strangely
enough, my essays may therefore be less dated than if I had
more closely followed the shifting trends of the decades.

The opening essay, which has given its title to the volume, is programmatic. It argues that the basic historical
fact in the life of Jesus is his death by execution as an
alleged king of the Jews. The conviction that the crucified
Messiah was vindicated by God who raised him from the dead
marks the beginning of Christianity and the central theme of
New Testament theology in all its complexity.

The three subsequent articles represent various approaches
which led to the conclusions drawn in the opening essay. "The
Messiahship of Jesus in Paul" deals with an often neglected aspect of Pauline theology and traces the lines backward. "The
Problem of the Historical Jesus" is a more general discussion
of historical method and Christian theology. The reader would
do well to observe that this paper was originally addressed to
a Scandinavian audience and published in Norwegian before Ernst
Käsemann's essay "The Historical Jesus" initiated a heated de-

bate to which I contributed by the opening essay of this volume.

The review article on Bultmann's Theology of the New Testament combines a critical analysis of the work with an attempt to explain its setting within the history of research. In doing so the article sets the stage for much recent work in this field, including my own efforts. I studied in Marburg during the summers 1936 and 1937. Later Bultmann himself asked me to write the review. Regretting that I did not feel more sympathy for his existential interpretation, he nevertheless praised it for its rare combination of understanding and critical distance.

The essay on "History and Eschatology" carries the discussion with Bultmann further and broadens the perspectives for my own approach. The final article, "The Atonement--An Adequate Reward for the Akedah?", further illustrates the interplay of historical data, interpretation of Scripture, and eschatological hopes. It shows that the story of the binding of Isaac was used, possibly already before Paul, to deal with the offense of a crucified Messiah.

I wish to dedicate this volume to my students, past and present. A number of them have long urged that some of my essays should be made readily available in English. Without their encouragement and assistance the volume would never have appeared. Fred Francis, Hiram Lester, Paul Sampley, and Bob Webber formed a first team of translators. Roger Aus prepared the translation of "History and Eschatology." Paul Donahue and Don Juel helped me to revise the translations and to make the manuscript ready for publication. I am also indebted to Augsburg Publishing House whose cooperation makes the fruits of common labor available to a wider public.

I cannot conclude this preface without once more recalling the summer in Marburg 1936. There I first met Birgit Rosencrantz. I have no words to express my thanks to her.

9

THE CRUCIFIED MESSIAH

Preliminary Questions

Few persons have made greater impact upon the history of
Norway than King Olav Haraldsson. The anniversary of his
death, July 29, is still celebrated in remembrance of the
introduction of Christianity. Olav was a Viking who, being
baptized, returned to the land of his fathers and became king.
With vigor and force he pursued the work of Christianizing and
unifying the land. The opposition to his brutal use of power
forced him to leave the country. In the year 1030 he returned
with an army, but fell at Stiklestad in a battle against the
peasants and local leaders, who on their part acknowledged the
lordship of King Knud of Denmark, also a Christian. On both
sides there were Christians as well as pagans; the war was
obviously a political one. And yet, scarcely had Olav fallen
when the belief arose that he had been a saint. In an amaz-
ingly short time the sentiment reversed among the people, the
leaders of the peasants did penance, the foreign sovereignty
was thrown off, and the work of Christianizing and unifying
the land was completed under the sign of the holy king and his
martyr-death. The figure operative in history, the originator
and bearer of the ensuing development, was Saint Olav, the rex
perpetuus Norvegiae, the Olav of saga and legend, of cultic
devotion and folk traditions. The "historical" Olav Digre
(i.e., Olav the Fat) is a critical-historical reconstruction
of nineteenth and twentieth century research.

It may be supposed that there must be something wrong in
the results of historical studies if no connection at all is
made visible which bridges the gap between the historical personality and the symbol of cult and ideology. But a gap, a

contrast, is in all events present. The tension between historical factuality and a historically operative symbol is a generally recognized phenomenon. From the perspectives of phenomenology and history of religions, the problem of "the historical Jesus and the kerygmatic Christ" will appear as a particular instance of this general phenomenon. As a matter of fact, the problem has been seen in this way by the "history of religions school," in which the Christ of the church was understood as a "cult-hero" and a "cult-symbol." The parallel with the holy king ought to have shown that the issues thus raised are only glossed over and not really solved by Martin Kähler's formula: not the so-called historical Jesus, but the biblical Christ is the eminently historical and the eminently real, since his figure alone has been operative in history.

In Norway, Olav and his death can be evaluated as national Christian symbols in the full consciousness that the historical figure as such was quite problematic. But with respect to Jesus Christ we are not in the same situation. The Christian faith hangs on the fact that Jesus Christ himself, and not merely a symbolic figure, encounters us in the preaching grounded in the apostolic testimony. It revolves not around the general problem of the relationship between a historical and a symbolic figure, but around the personal identity of the Christ exalted to the right hand of the Father with the Jesus of Nazareth who was crucified under Pontius Pilate. This identity was also for Kähler the genuine concern, and his criticism of the biographies of Jesus was indeed relevant not only for dogmatics but also for historical studies. But Kähler's conviction of faith was clothed in the not-entirely appropriate garb of the philosophy of history and of apologetics. Thus it was not made clear that the New Testament itself shows that the biblical picture of Jesus was historically not the only possible one.

11

Pilate, the chief priests, the Pharisees, and also the disciples in the time before the passion understood Jesus differently and did not have the same picture of him as the disciples after Easter. The possibility of offense was always present. What is necessary to faith is not a basis in scientific or philosophical interpretations of history, but simply the possibility to face all the historical facts of the case openly and without apologetic manipulations and then not to take offense. Thus a sober historical approach is required, one that can contribute to a clarification of the implications of the decision of faith without taking away from man the responsibility for his own decision.

Thus I see the primary task of research concerning the historical Jesus to be that of laying bare, as far as possible, what really happened. This question and the question "how it really was" are certainly not as plain and simple as they once seemed. For what does "really" mean? Is the real what is in the foreground, substantiated by everyone? Or is it much more what is in the background, the real significance of what has been and happened? Bruta facta as such are not yet real history, for to human history there always belongs the interpretation of what happened, even when it is the interpretation of the historian asking about the facts and explaining them. The proper discretion of the historian emerges when he does not forceably impose his own interpretation upon the material, but rather strives to bring to expression the material standing at his disposal.[1] The historian must always allow his own understanding, without which he cannot work at all, to be enriched and corrected by being open to interpretations that have been given to the events by men who share in them and have been shaped by them. But the historical and real should not be identified with the historically operative, and scholarly discretion is not to be understood as anxiety in the face of radical questions.

These few remarks may be sufficient to outline my approach to the question of the history of Jesus. By means of methodological and theological considerations, and also by philosophical reflection upon the idea of history, this question could be pursued much further than is possible here. Nevertheless, it must be said that the really burning questions cannot be answered in principle but only through constant new encounters with the material. The clarification of conceptions and of basic questions serves a purpose for research only insofar as work with the text and with particular problems is thereby advanced. From time to time the great and fundamental questions must be asked; in this way blind alleys are exposed, false questions and alternatives are unmasked, and new ways are opened for further research. But it is seldom fruitful to dwell too long on discussions of methodology and principles. It was very necessary and very useful that some years ago the problem of the historical Jesus was raised anew.[2] Now it seems to me the time has come when we would do better to turn again to work with specific questions.

The question of the relation between the proclaimed Christ and the historical Jesus cannot be answered simply by confronting the post-Easter proclamation with the preaching and conduct of Jesus before his passion. Between these the death of Jesus stands as a decisive event. The death of Jesus is at the center of the church's proclamation and is precisely the point at which the historical quest for the life of Jesus must start.[3] How is it possible to believe in the death of Jesus as the ground of our salvation and at the same time to make the death of Jesus the object of historical-critical research? And what is the relation between what we are able to

13

say about it as historians and what we as members of the church confess and preach? Many questions arise, of which I select one: the question of the meaning and legitimacy of saying that Jesus has been crucified as the Messiah.

Creedal Summaries

The New Testament proclaims the death of Jesus as the death of Christ, the messianic salvation-event. Outside the Gospels, the historical particulars of the passion narrative are seldom mentioned. Allusions are found almost exclusively in the kerygmatic summaries in Acts. This fact, however, is not only due to the historicizing tendency of Luke, but also to the difference between missionary preaching and hymnic-liturgical formulations (cf. also 1 Cor. 15:3ff. and 1 Thess. 2:15f.). The death of Jesus as an act of men can be contrasted with his resurrection as an act of God. When the responsibility of the Jews is stressed and the complicity of the Romans is allowed to go largely unnoticed, it is less for political-apologetic motives than for a conception of salvation history in which the Jews' responsibility was the significant fact, at first for preaching salvation and repentance to the Jews and later for the church in its relation to the Old Testament and to the synagogue.

The plot against Jesus can be attributed to Satan (John 13:27; 14:30; cf. Luke 22:3, 53), and the lords of this world appear as the executors of the crucifixion (1 Cor. 2:8). In this way the cosmic, supernatural dimensions of the event are indicated. The conceptions are not really mythological since Satan and the powers do not act directly but through men. Elsewhere the death of Jesus appears as an act of God, who employed the adversaries as his instruments without their knowledge or will in order to realize his secret design. Luke

14

reconciles the different aspects by emphasizing that the Jews acted according to the design and predetermination of God (Acts 2:23; 4:28). Other writers only stress what was of theological significance: the death of Jesus is the revelation of God's saving righteousness and the act of his love (Rom. 3:25; 5:8; 2 Cor. 5:16, 21; 1 John 4:9f.). However, this in no way denies that the crucifixion was an act of men and a historical fact. In John this paradox is expressed by means of the Jews being able to appear as the instigators of the "lifting up" of Jesus (John 8:28).

The relation between historical and theological aspects is more difficult to determine in those statements in which the death of Christ appears not as a passive but as an active deed. Here a whole series of images and figures is employed: Jesus has laid down his life and thereby brought about a ransom. He has on his own authority offered his life for us. Through death he has consecrated and sacrificed himself. He has overcome hostility and made peace. Through his death he has triumphed over death and the devil. Through death and exaltation he has gone to the Father. As high priest he has entered the heavenly sanctuary. Such are obviously not historical statements about phenomena that can be observed and substantiated. Furthermore, they do not claim to be. Their subject matter is rather the mystery of Jesus' death, the significance of which cannot be confirmed historically but can be preached, confessed and praised only through faith in the Resurrected One. The death of Jesus appears as a saving event only in its unity with the resurrection, mediated through the word of reconciliation that is instituted by the Resurrected One.

Jesus' act of dying can also be conceived in ethical categories such as endurance, obedience, and love. But it is

rather striking in this regard that precisely the dogmatic,
hymnic-doxological texts speak about this, while the more historical reports of the gospels maintain a modest silence about
Jesus' disposition during his passion; only a glimmer of it can
be seen between the lines. Where the language is direct and
open about the forbearance of the suffering Christ, it nearly
always occurs in connection with the Old Testament (1 Peter
1:22ff.; Rom. 15:3; indeed also Heb. 5:7f.). The obedience of
Jesus appears as the eschatological counterpart to the fall of
Adam (Rom. 5:19) or as an extension of the self-renunciation
of the pre-existent Christ who divested himself of his equality
with God (Phil. 2:6ff.). The death of Jesus is an act of his
love; but the love of Christ is not to be understood psycho-
logically, but rather the contrary: since the death of Jesus
is proclaimed and believed as a saving event, it is also understood as perfect obedience and as an act of love. "Love is
visible only to faith in it."[4] This applies in a special way
to the love of Christ shown on the cross in its identity with
the love of God.

Like the saving significance of the cross, so also the
sinlessness and the forbearance, the love and obedience of the
crucified are not historically verifiable phenomena. This fact
is not first of all a "given" to which modern historians must
resign themselves; rather it is already apparent from the very
manner in which the New Testament authors use a language of
confession and praise when they speak about the obedience and
love of Christ. In the statements that are to be theologically
and soteriologically understood, however, the historical is not
excluded but included. This is true where the death of Jesus
is spoken of as an act of God as well as where it is seen as
manifesting the forbearing, obedient, and loving character of
Jesus Christ. The proclamation and the confessing praise

presuppose that the conduct of Jesus, visible to men, can be understood as an expression for and an indication of the fact that here Christ, the Son of God, suffered for our sakes--not, to be sure, that it must be so understood; that which is historical remains ambiguous. If the interpretation were correct that Jesus actually was a political insurgent and was rightly executed as such and that the end of his life broke in upon him as a completely unforeseen catastrophe, then that would in fact be fatal for faith in the Christ proclaimed in the New Testament. Thus, what is historically identifiable certainly has no constitutive significance for preaching and faith, but it is not irrelevant. This is shown also by the fact that beside the christological hymns and formulas of the New Testament stand the passion narratives of the gospels.

The Passion Narratives

The passion stories are in the form of narrative accounts of what happened. This does not mean that the purely historical viewpoint was the overriding and controlling one. The evangelists and the bearers of the traditions before them participate with their whole beings in what is told here. That they tell, what they tell, and how they tell the story--all is determined by their faith in the Crucified One who is the resurrected Christ. The kerygmatic-doxological statements in the rest of the New Testament imply the historical facts; a theological significance is no less implicit in the passion narratives of the Gospels. This significance is only infrequently expressed, but it determines the entire manner of the telling. In each of the four evangelists one may speak of something like a theology of the passion story.[5] The evangelists bear witness, each in his own way, that on Golgotha has occurred the decisive event in the history of God's dealing with man.

17

The concern of the evangelists--kerygmatic, cultic, de-
votional, or whatever one wishes to call it--carries with it
both the retention of the events in memory and a transformation of the historical picture. The passion narratives contain features that are to be characterized as legendary not
only in a form-critical but also negatively in a historical
sense. But they also contain historical facts. The dispute
arises over the degree to which the one and the other element
are present.

Various motifs within the passion narratives can be distinguished: proof from prophecy, apologetics, novelistic
features, moral injunctions, dogmatic and cultic interests,
and the like.[6] However, neither stylistically nor in content
is there any success with a pure separation between what is
historical, legendary, or dogmatic. All such elements are
intertwined; the historical is not merely historical, the
theological not dogmatic and rational. As a whole and in its
parts the passion story is condensed in content and symboli-
cally powerful. The very way it is presented expresses the
inner participation of the narrator and the hidden dimension
of what happened.

With reference to the creed-like statements about the
death of Christ the expression "pathos-formula" has been employed.[7] The designation is not an entirely fitting one.
Form-critically it is unclear, and with respect to content it
is not wholly appropriate. But it does render one service:
it expresses our failure in the use of precise categories of
style, content, and function. As in the "liturgical" formulas
so also in the passion narratives, we must be aware of the
"pathos" in order to discover what is at stake. Pathos is
missing in none of the evangelists, but it is strongest in
Mark, no doubt because he depicts the passion story with blunt

18

realism without alluding to the latent authority of the Son of God in the direct dogmatic manner of Matthew and John and also without highlighting the nobility in the suffering of the perfect martyr as in Luke.

None of the evangelists has recounted the passion story without pathos, disinterestedly, like a neutral reporter. But, although the historical interest at no time becomes an end in itself, it is still present. Mark cites authorities (14:51; 15:21); he gives information about what motivated the opponents of Jesus (15:10; cf. 12:12-13), how it happened that Jesus was arrested alone and without greater sensation (14:1-4, 10f., 43ff.), and upon what juridical basis he was condemned (14:55ff.; 15:2). Whether or not he has given the historically correct answers, he is moved by the question of what happened and how it came about. In Matthew it is not very different. In the passion narrative also, Luke emerges as the "historian" among the evangelists; with him it is clear that Jesus must be accused before Pilate as a political insurgent (23:2, 5, 14). It is more noteworthy that also the fourth evangelist--and he in particular--strives to set forth clearly the causal connections that led to Jesus' death. Perhaps even more than in Luke, the political aspects of the trial are given special prominence (John 11:45ff., 57; 12:10f., 17ff.; 18:13f., 19f., 29ff.; 19:6ff.). It is questionable to what extent Luke and John have at their disposal historical reports which go beyond Mark. If they do not, these two evangelists exhibit an all the more notable sense of history.

From a literary point of view, the passion narratives are characterized by the tension between events in the foreground that can be observed by all and their mysterious background, that which happened within what happened.[8] Concealed within the earthly event is the mystery of God, which first became

manifest to the disciples through the appearances of the resurrected Christ in order that it might be revealed through
their preaching. In John the distinction between outward hap-
penings and their deeper significance is explicitly stressed.
It is a political comment in the mouth of the high priest that
it would be better that one man die for the people than that
the whole nation perish. Without knowing it, however, the
high priest thus speaks as a prophet of the vicarious suffering of Christ (John 11:49ff.). Pilate formulates the title on
the cross in order to annoy the Jews, but the inscription in
three languages proclaim for all the world that the one crucified is the "King of the Jews," the promised Messiah (John
19:19ff.). This is also the meaning in the synoptics, even if
it is not as clearly expressed. The accusation against Jesus
is understood in the passion narratives as an indirect testimony that the crucified is the Christ, while in the passion
formulas he is directly proclaimed and praised as such.

The engagement of faith and the pathos of the account thus
does not exclude a historical interest on the part of the evangelists, but rather includes it. This interest is interwoven
with the concern of faith, but it is not completely one with
it. The mystery, the death of Jesus as a saving event, is only
to be grasped in faith, which is always at the same time faith
in the resurrected Christ. A fact that can be historically
confirmed can belong only to the foreground of the event. However, to ask also about such things is not illegitimate for
the Christian. What was first held together in the pathos of
the passion narratives becomes separated for us who belong to
a later, sophisticated generation: here confession, preaching,
and faith, there historical research. We can only pursue the
historical interest as we work critically and avail ourselves
of all means and methods of historical study at our disposal.

An Unsettled Question of Albert Schweitzer

It cannot be said in advance how far it will be possible
to obtain a certain, unambiguous answer to our historical
question: What really happened in the death of Jesus? How
did the course of events lead to the condemnation? What
circumstances, motives, and contributing causes were of significance? What light does the death of Jesus shed upon his
previous life and his preaching? In any case it should be
possible to make some advances, for in reality little has been
done with these questions in the last decades. This is a result of misgivings about the nineteenth century biographies of
Jesus, but is not a legitimate consequence of the reaction
against them. For the historical question about the death of
Jesus in its relation to his previous life was not settled by
the demise of psychologizing biographies; rather it became
acute. Albert Schweitzer had asked this question in his
"Sketch of the Life of Jesus," which originated in connection
with a work on the Lord's Supper.[9] Later he formulated it
clearly and powerfully in his debate with Wrede, even if his
answer was no more than an arbitrary conjecture.[10]

A new quest for the historical Jesus cannot simply and
unreflectively continue or resume the line of the old biographical research without an awareness of the insights for
which we are obliged to, among others, Kähler and form criticism. However, we should not be induced--perhaps by a new
conception of history--to overlook our obligations to take up
anew genuine, unsolved problems of the older research. Recent
research has unjustly taken up from Schweitzer only the problem of eschatology and the "delay of the parousia," but not at
the same time the chief problem with regard to Jesus' life,
namely, the problem of the non-messianic character of Jesus'
public ministry in relation to his messiahship affirmed by the

sources. Schweitzer's main asset as a New Testament critic
lay in his ability, trained through the history of research,
to see essential problems and to ask sharp questions. Nineteenth century German research into the life of Jesus had a
double outcome: Wrede and Schweitzer. The correspondence and
the difference between the two types of solutions led Schweitzer to formulate the alternatives: "The inconsistency between
the public life of Jesus and his Messianic claim lies either
in the nature of the Jewish Messianic conception, or in the
representation of the Evangelist. . . . Tertium non datur."[11]

Contemporary research has scarcely gone beyond these
alternatives, although the literary analysis and tradition-
criticism following Wrede have become keener and more penetrating (Bultmann, and others), while the interpretation of the
self-consciousness of Jesus in light of Jewish messianic ideas
has been carried on with more learning and greater circumspec-
tion than in Schweitzer (e.g., by Joachim Jeremias and Erik
Sjöberg). The advocates of the two typical solutions have
appealed to good arguments and have been able to point out the
difficulties in the opposing attempts at solutions. Therefore
the discussion has not come to an end. But at the same time,
both sides have a common difficulty. In the early Christian
confession and kerygma Jesus was proclaimed as the anointed
one (Messiah, Christos). This fact cannot be easily accounted
for either by supposing that Jesus in no sense intended to be
the Messiah or by assuming that he combined in his own person
the role of heavenly Son of Man with that of Suffering Servant.
Does there exist a third possibility beyond the alternative
explanations in terms of community dogmatic or Jewish messianism?

The Inscription of the Charge

In this connection it is essential to determine if Jesus was actually crucified as a messianic pretender, as the evangelists say. This is contested by Bultmann, for example, who asserts that Jesus was condemned and executed not as Messiah but as a messianic prophet; the view that Jesus should die as Messiah belongs to the dogmatic motifs of the passion story.[12] The motif is undoubtedly dogmatic, but must it therefore be unhistorical? This question cannot be answered by a priori considerations. Historically both alternatives are conceivable: Jesus could have been crucified either as a messianic pretender or as a false prophet and agitator. The motif is firmly anchored in the sources. To be sure, one cannot argue on the basis of the proceedings before the Sanhedrin (Mark 14:55ff. par.), for its historicity is indeed questionable. Moreover, Bultmann may be right that the accusation in Mark 15:2 is a secondary expansion parallel to 15:3-5. But this does not prove that the inscription of the charge in 15:26 is also secondary.[13] It is more probable that the question of 15:2 was formulated in view of the inscription "King of the Jews," which is firmly fixed in the tradition. Further, this title occurs in the Barabbas episode and in the scene where the soldiers do mock-homage to Jesus; it is presupposed in the reviling of the crucified (Mark 15:9, 12, 16ff., 32). This is not very easy to explain if the motif is really secondary.

Mark's presentation is confirmed by the fact that the crucifixion of Jesus as "King of the Jews" is also a chief motif of the Johannine passion narrative, which, on the whole, is not dependent upon the synoptics (cf. John 18:33ff.; 19:1-3, 12-15, 19-22).[14] Thus in any case the motif must be very old. John gives it a spiritualized meaning; in Matthew and Luke it is less prominent than in Mark.[15] The formulation "King of

23

the Jews" stems neither from proof from prophecy nor from the Christology of the community. In general early Christians hesitated to use the title "King" for Jesus. Would the formulation of the inscription, with its decidedly political ring, really rest on a historicization of a dogmatic motif? This is not very plausible. It is difficult to imagine a form of the passion story that was merely a historical report in no way speaking of the messiahship of the crucified. Thus in any case the crucified Messiah motif belongs to the substance of the passion story, though its historicity is still not proved.

The Christianizing of the Title Messiah

There is another consideration which is decisive: That the title Messiah was inextricably bound up with the name of Jesus can only be explained by presupposing that Jesus was actually crucified as the Messiah. Otherwise one falls into great difficulties and cannot make historically understandable the title's Christian meaning and its wide use as another name of Jesus.[16] At this point I can only sketch the results of more extensive work. In all the writings in the New Testament Jesus is proclaimed as the Christ. But the name Christ is not the expression of any particular christological conception but is rather a common denominator for the various conceptions that are found in the New Testament. In the oldest sources, the Pauline epistles, Christos always denotes the one Christ, Jesus. It is not a colorless proper name, however, but an honorific designation, whose content is supplied by the person and work of Jesus Christ. Where Christos appears as a more general term for the Messiah announced in the Old Testament, there are often signs of later theologizing, which is also to be seen in patristic literature. For example, in Luke, as in Justin, the primitive kerygma, "Christ died. . . according to

24

the scriptures," has developed into two statements: "the
anointed one must suffer," and, "Jesus is the anointed one."
Actually, what these writers and many after them present as
the Old Testament doctrine of the Messiah has been conformed
to their image of Jesus the Christ.

Thus from the beginnings of Greek-speaking Christianity--
within a few years of the crucifixion--the name Christ as
applied to Jesus must have been firmly established. This presupposes that Jesus was already designated "the Messiah" and
"Jesus the Messiah" in the Aramaic-speaking regions. To this
extent the Christology of the primitive community from the
very first must have been a Messiah-Christology. To be sure,
Jesus was also spoken of as "Son of Man" and "Servant of God,"
but these designations never appear as predicates. In the
kerygma and confession it is not "Jesus is the Son of Man" or
"Jesus is the Servant of God," but always "Jesus is the Messiah," and further, "Jesus is the Son of God" or "Jesus is the
Kyrios." The content of the predicate Messiah was determined
essentially by the crucifixion and resurrection of Jesus and
only to a limited extent by a previous conception of the Messiah.

From the very first, faith in Jesus as the Resurrected
One was faith in him as the Messiah. This is not to be explained by the Easter event alone. To a Jew of Jesus' time
the ideas were not completely foreign that a man be raised
from the dead or be exalted to heaven; likewise a person of
the past could return at the end time. Such statements might
apply to Enoch, Elijah, perhaps also to Moses, Melchizedek
and others (cf. also Mark 6:14ff.; 8:28). However, none of
this in itself has anything to do with the Messiah or messiahship. From the discovery of the empty tomb (if it is historical) and from the appearances of the Resurrected One it could

be inferred that Jesus lives and is exalted to heaven. But
from this it could not be inferred that he is the Messiah. In
the resurrection stories in the Gospels the messiahship of
Jesus is not especially stressed apart from specifically Lukan
formulations (Luke 24:26, 46).[17] The resurrection does mean,
however, that Jesus was vindicated by God _vis-a-vis_ his adversaries. If he was crucified as an alleged Messiah, then—but
only then—does faith in his resurrection necessarily become
faith in the resurrection of the crucified Messiah. In this
way the distinctiveness of the Christian idea of the Messiah,
in contrast to the Jewish, was given from the outset. Whether
it is said that God will send the foreordained Messiah, Jesus
(Acts 3:20f.), or that Jesus is enthroned as Messiah (Acts
2:36), or that Christ died for our sins (1 Cor. 15:3) is a
matter of minor importance in this context.

Jewish messianic expectations do not explain the meaning
of the name Messiah assigned to Jesus. Neither can it be said
that the title Messiah is the necessary contemporary expression for the conviction that Jesus is the eschatological
bringer of salvation. This is no more valid than the older
assertion that messiahship was the necessary garb for the ar-
chetypical religious self-consciousness of Jesus. Jewish
eschatology did not know just one salvation figure; in addition
to the royal Messiah there was the eschatological high priest,
the prophet like Moses, Elijah _redivivus_, the warrior from
Ephraim; and there were still other figures. The expectation,
as we now see clearly, was not systematized so that the other
figures were taken as forerunners of the true Messiah; instead
they were parallel figures. What remained constant were the
eschatologically interpreted statements of the scriptures; on
particular questions exegesis had its freedom. Scriptural
passages could be connected in various ways, and certain fig-

26

ures are combined and even identified with each other; they
could also go unnoticed.

Rarely has it been made clear how strange it is that precisely the title Messiah was applied to Jesus and became his
name. The title stems from that figure in Jewish eschatology
that has almost nothing at all in common with the New Testament picture of Christ. "The Messiah," used absolutely as an
eschatological term, designates the political Messiah, the
king of the house of David. Accordingly, in the New Testament
Christos is in more than one place a synonym for "King of
Israel" (or "King of the Jews"), while nowhere is it necessary
to presuppose another significance. And since it is not necessary, it should not be done. Now it may indeed be supposed
that in popular piety, as in the synagogue prayers, the Messi-
ah-King was the dominant figure; this is also the figure for
which the broadest basis is to be found in Holy Scripture.
The first Christians, however, found prophecy of the Christ
neither exclusively nor even principally in the parts of the
Old Testament that were interpreted messianically in the nar-
row sense in Judaism.[18] Not only were the prophecies about
the Son of David referred to the Messiah Jesus; testimonies to
him were also found in the texts about the prophet like Moses,
the eschatological high priest, the Son of Man, the Servant of
the Lord, the messenger of salvation (Isa. 52), the pierced
one (Zech. 12), and in many passages that in Judaism were not
at all interpreted as referring to an eschatological figure.
If the prophecies in Malachi 3 were not often referred to
Jesus, it is only because John the Baptist had already been
identified--by Jesus himself (?)--with the coming Elijah.[19]

Jesus' name, Messiah, surely implies that in him and
through him the promises of God were fulfilled; but in this no
special thought was given to the specifically messianic proph-

27

ecies of the Old Testament. But this means that the application of the title Messiah to Jesus cannot have had its origin in the study of scripture and in the discussion of the first Christians with Jews. Both are only secondary factors. The messiahship of the crucified Jesus is rather the presupposition that lies at the root of all the scriptural evidence de Christo. Since the central place of the name Messiah cannot be explained from the preaching of Jesus, there remains only one possibility: the title Messiah was inseparably connected with the name of Jesus because Jesus was condemned and crucified as a messianic pretender.

We may now draw two important conclusions. 1. That Jesus was crucified as King of the Jews is not a dogmatic motif that has become historicized in the passion narratives; precisely to the contrary, it is a historical fact that became centrally important for the formulation of the first Christian dogma: Jesus is the Messiah. 2. The confession of Jesus as the Messiah is not to be understood as a "rejudaizing" of the preaching and person of Jesus, but on the contrary as a thorough, radical Christianizing of the Jewish title of Messiah.

The Gospels and the Messiahship of Jesus

From what precedes, the data given by the evangelists can be evaluated. They too presuppose the concept Christos as reinterpreted in Christian terms. Only in a few places is the name put into the mouth of Jesus (Matt. 23:10; Mark 9:41; John 17:3). Matthew makes rather extensive use of the Christian concept of Messiah in the gospel story. Luke characteristically speaks in Old Testament language about Jesus as God's anointed. A knowledge of the contrast between Jewish messianic doctrine and New Testament faith in Christ is most clearly expressed in John.[20] As a general conception not directly

28

applied to Jesus, _Christos_ appears in the question about the
Messiah as son and as Lord of David (Mark 12:35-37 par.) as
well as in the prophecy about false christs coming forward
(Mark 13:21 par.). It seems certain that before the passion
Jesus did not openly claim to be the Messiah.

Matthew understands Peter's confession at Caesarea Philip-
pi as a prototype of the Christian confession of Christ. But
this is a secondary interpretation.[21] Mark's version must be
read in light of the themes of the messianic secret and of the
disciple's misunderstanding. Peter speaks the truth; Jesus is
indeed the Christ. But Peter does not yet understand the implications of this truth. He cannot accept the idea of the
passion because he sees in Jesus the Messiah (contrast in Matthew). This means that, according to Mark, Peter still understands the name Messiah in a Jewish sense. A beatitude addressed to Peter would be impossible in Mark; the true messiahship of Jesus remains a secret even to the disciples until
the passion and resurrection. Furthermore, the Markan form of
the pericope is a composition in which a motif appearing elsewhere has been used (Mark 8:28-6:14f.). But it may be a historical recollection that even in his lifetime Jesus was "one
who was hoped to be the Messiah, but who not only at the moment of failure, but in his entire message and ministry, disappointed the hopes that were placed in him."[22]

May we suppose that Jesus himself gave a new interpretation to the concept of Messiah? For this assumption there is
really only one piece of evidence, the question about the son
of David (Mark 12:35-37). In it is contained an indirect messianic claim. The answer to the problem of the seemingly self-
contradictory statements of scripture lies in the concrete
messiahship of Jesus who, as a man, is son of David but as the
Exalted One is his Lord. Here the Christian concept of Messi-

29

ah is indeed presupposed. And for precisely this reason the
pericope is probably a product of Christian scriptural interpretation. It belongs to those elements of the tradition
whose historicity cannot be demonstrated because of their
close conformity to the kerygma of the church.[23]

The designation Son of Man in Jesus' words in the Gospels
is and remains enigmatic, no less so because the pre-Christian
origin of the figurative language of the Book of Enoch has now
once again become doubtful. If I am right that the name Messiah must have stood at the center of the early community's
confession and preaching, it becomes impossible to consider
all the traditional Son of Man sayings as constructions of the
community. A kernel of traditional, genuine Son of Man sayings must have existed as a point of departure for the Gospels'
widespread use of Son of Man as Jesus' self-designation.[24]
But this does not prove that Jesus, drawing upon peculiar
apocalyptic traditions, understood himself as the hidden Son
of Man. In the words of Jesus most widely accepted as authentic, either the Son of Man is an eschatological figure not
clearly identified with Jesus (Mark 8:38 and par.) or Jesus
speaks of himself non-eschatologically as Son of Man, i.e., as
an individual man. Thus in the latter case it is not clear
that he claims to be the Son of Man of Daniel 7 (Matt. 8:20 Q;
11:19 Q). Those passion predictions which might most plausi-
bly be considered authentic are not joined to any titles.[25]

Did Jesus think that he was the eschatological Son of Man?
Criticism and exegesis of the words of Jesus transmitted by
tradition cannot answer this or the more general question of
messianic self-consciousness with certainty. The Gospels were
written by men who believed that Jesus was the Christ, the Messiah as Christians understood that term. The preserved Son of
Man sayings have been interpreted from this perspective. But

in themselves they are remarkably ambiguous. Negatively it
can be maintained that Jesus before his passion made no express
and unequivocal claim to messiahship (cf. John 10:24f.). But
does this exclude the possibility that in some sense he thought
himself the Messiah? Positively it can be said that if Jesus
regarded himself as Messiah, "he thought of his messiahship
essentially in the categories of an apocalyptic conception of
the Son of Man," though admittedly he transformed the apocalyptic image he appropriated.[26] But is this presupposition
correct? Can any advance toward the solution of this problem
so vexing for contemporary research be made if we begin with
the idea that the crucifixion of Jesus as messianic pretender
must be taken to be a historical fact? It is along this
course that we must proceed.

Of course, caution is needed. I agree with Käsemann that
we cannot reconstruct a life of Jesus since we do not have the
requisite knowledge of his external and psychological development.[27] But from this it does not follow that historical
questions about causal relationships neither can nor ought be
asked at all. Questions about the causes and effects of Jesus'
death may certainly be purposefully asked; moreover, they must
be asked, whether we find the task pleasant or not. Answers
can only be given incompletely and approximately, the best
claim can only be to a high degree of probability. But this
is not only because of the nature of the sources but just as
much because of the general problems that are bound up with
the use of causal explanations in historical research. Nevertheless the historian cannot completely renounce the application of the concept of causality.[28]

We know little with certainty about the motives that led
the authorities to take legal steps against Jesus. But we can
conjecture some things with good reason: Jesus' sovereign

31

attitude to the prescriptions of the law, his relation to the
poor and to many suspect individuals, and especially his public appearance in the temple--all this, in conjunction with
his eschatological preaching, could appear to be a revolt
against the established religio-political order. The messianic hopes of Jesus' followers may have been sufficient to
occasion the charges raised against him. With Bornkamm we
have to speak "not of Jesus' non-messianic history before his
passion, but indeed of a movement of broken messianic hopes."[29]

The fact that Jesus was arrested alone is one indication
among others that there can be no serious question of a messi-
anic-political movement under Jesus' leadership (in spite of
Robert Eisler, among others). Jesus was crucified as a messianic pretender, but he did not himself claim to be the Messiah,
at least not publicly. A. Schweitzer wanted to explain this
apparent contradiction by assuming that Judas betrayed the
messianic secret. This theory was a necessity for Schweitzer's
whole construction, but it belongs in the realm of historical
fiction. From Jesus' crucifixion as "King of the Jews" no
direct conclusions can be drawn about Jesus' messianic self-
consciousness before the Passion. To be sure, Jesus' activities are likely to have given rise to the question, among both
followers and opponents, whether or not he thought himself to
be the Messiah. The authority with which he invested his actions makes this understandable. But it must have been his
opponents who put messiahship in the foreground and made it
the decisive question of life and death. It is very doubtful
that a precise historical report lies behind the synoptic account of the proceedings before the Sanhedrin. The essential
point, however, would seem to be historically accurate. The
inscription of charge presupposes that Jesus was accused before
Pilate on the ground that he made a royal-messianic claim. If

so, one may further infer that Jesus, confronted with that charge that he thought himself to be the Messiah, accepted the accuracy of the charge by his silence, if not in any other way.[30]

The claim to be the Messiah was thus extorted from Jesus. He did not raise it on his own initiative--at least not expressly and directly. However, before the accusation made in the face of impending death, he did not deny he was the Messiah. From this, one might try to argue back to a previous messianic consciousness and perhaps find a point of contact in possible Jewish ideas about a suffering Messiah. But the line of argument is uncertain. We may say with greater confidence that Jesus could not deny the charge that he was the Messiah without thereby putting in question the final, eschatological validity of his whole message and ministry. Further, it may be said that willingness to suffer is implicit in Jesus' behavior and attitude throughout his preaching.[31] This was verified by his willingness to die a rejected and ridiculed Messiah. We are able to say almost nothing at all from a psychological viewpoint about Jesus' attitude during the passion. But we may take it as a historical fact that Jesus did nothing to avoid his condemnation and crucifixion as "King of the Jews." Only in the form of this "good confession" before Pontius Pilate does a "messianic claim" of Jesus become historically accessible. But this is precisely the one thing that is a necessary presupposition for the New Testament gospel of the crucified Messiah.

Concluding Remarks

The contradiction between Jesus' non-messianic public appearances and his messiahship is to be explained neither from the nature of Jewish messianic ideas nor by the tension

between historical facts and the conceptions of the evangelists. There is a third possibility. Indeed many things can
and must be explained by analysis of sources and traditions,
and it is conceivable that Jesus appropriated certain ideas of
Jewish messianism. The real explanation, however, is to be
sought in the historical event itself; the inconsistency stems
from Jesus' crucifixion as the Messiah despite the fact that
he never made an express messianic claim. He did not deny the
accusation that he acted the role of Messiah when it was raised
against him. This fact had a determinative significance for
the Christian kerygma and thus for the ideas of the evangelists. The end of Jesus' life stands at the heart of the gospel; the historical Jesus like the kerygmatic Christ is the
crucified Messiah.

There is no gap between the historical Jesus and the
preaching of the church; rather there exists a close and in-
separable connection. We have not achieved this result by
abstracting from historical matters of fact in order to ask
only about the "continuity of the gospel in the discontinuity
of the times" (Käsemann). Nor is this to say that we have
reckoned with a conception of Heilsgeschichte with its own
laws and its own continuity detached from general history.
Rather, the question has been simply historical, and the continuity that I see is first of all a historical, causal continuity. This continuity is not purely theological or ideologi-
cal; the church's preaching of Christ is not to be traced back
to the self-consciousness of Jesus or to his preaching. What
we have found is rather a complex series of actions and reactions of various people who were involved in the events. Not
only the conduct of Jesus and his disciples, but also that of
Caiaphas and Pilate was of decisive significance. What applies
to the external course of the events is also true for the theo-

34

logical interpretation. The formulation of the confession presupposes the formulation of the charge and was occasioned by it.
It is quite probable that the title Messiah was first brought
forth as an expression of false expectation, as an accusation
and as a mockery of Jesus. Only later, after the appearances
of the Risen Lord, was it taken up as a unifying expression of
confession and preaching. With this the ambiguity of the historical continuity becomes quite clear. Only by faith in the
resurrection has the scandal of the crucified Messiah been
overcome.

The preaching of the resurrected Christ still makes the
death of Jesus a saving event for us. The truth of the gospel
does not permit validation through historical investigation.
However, it seems arbitrary to isolate the message and the
life of Jesus from his death as the crucified Messiah in order
to seek the essence of Christianity in the "so-called historical Jesus" isolated in such a way. I find it equally impossible to see historical research as something standing beside
the kerygma with parallel access to the significance of Jesus,
unless the crucifixion should finally become a dispensable
symbol for the proper understanding of existence. Insofar as
this is true, faith remains directed toward the preached, biblical Christ. But this does not lead us to escape the difficulties bound up with the question of the historical Jesus;
the kerygma is much too closely involved with the historical
events for that to happen.

I am somewhat sceptical of slogans and great syntheses.
If the proposal sketched here has worth, it is this: an important single question--the historical problem of the application of the title Messiah to Jesus--has been clearly asked
and to some extent precisely answered. Some guiding principles and consequences have been laid out, but no final answers

attained; old problems are cast in a new light and broader
questions raised. Thus the result is shown to be a genuinely
historical one. Such a clarification--of what lends itself
to historical clarification--should not be unwelcome to faith
in the preached Jesus Christ.[32]

THE MESSIAHSHIP OF JESUS IN PAUL

Paul's Christology can be stated almost without referring to the messiahship of Jesus. Nevertheless, one will scarcely deny that the question whether Jesus was the Messiah or not was crucial in the life of the one-time persecutor and later apostle. The problem of this apparent contradiction is often too quickly bypassed. It is hoped that a few observations and reflections of a philological, historical, and theological nature will contribute to the clarification of the problem.

Philological Observations

The philological question concerns the meaning of the word Christos. Is the name still employed by Paul as a title or is it only a proper name?[1] Preliminary study leads to the following negative conclusions:

1. In the Pauline letters Christos is never a general term but always a designation for the one Christ, Jesus (on the contrary see Acts 17:3; 26:23).

2. Christos is never used as a predicate; Paul never says, "Jesus is the Christ," or the like (otherwise Acts 18:5, 28).

3. A genitive is never added; Paul does not say, "the Christ of God."

4. The form Iēsous ho Christos is not to be found in the oldest text of the epistles (against this 1 Cor. 3:11 TR).

In order to understand the sense of the apostle's statements, it is not necessary for Paul's readers to know that Christos is a term filled with content and pregnant with meaning. Even if one understands Christ only to be a surname of Jesus, all the statements of the epistles make good sense.

This does not exclude the possibility that the name "Christ"
bears a fullness of meaning. However, the messiahship of
Jesus is not stressed.

Nonetheless, the name "Christ" is not completely fixed as
a proper name. This is supported by the use of the forms
Christos Iēsous and Iēsous Christos interchangeably.[2] Further-
more, it is clear that Iēsous has remained Jesus' proper name.
The confession reads: "Jesus is Lord (Rom. 10:9; 1 Cor. 12:3)
or "Jesus Christ is Lord" (Phil. 2:11), but not "Christ is
Lord." Elsewhere Paul speaks of the Lord Jesus or the Lord
Jesus Christ, but not of the Lord Christ. Romans 16:18 and
Colossians 3:24 constitute only apparent exceptions since both
contrast serving the Lord who is Christ to serving other lords.

Paul says "Christ" and "the Christ," as well as "Jesus
Christ" and "Christ Jesus." The varying forms are fixed by
grammatical and stylistic considerations as well as by habits
of speech. As a rule a simple form, either "Christ," "the
Christ," or "the Lord," stands as the subject of a sentence.[3]
Those complete, liturgical-sounding forms, such as "(our) Lord
Jesus Christ" are used primarily in the genitive and in prepo-
sitional phrases and occur frequently at the end of a sentence.[4] Moreover, Paul always writes (ho) kyrios (hēmōn)
Iēsous Christos, but if the name "Lord" follows he alternates
between "Jesus Christ" and "Christ Jesus." Furthermore, Paul
obviously avoids the dative form, Iēsou, which is identical
with the genitive; for that reason Christ is placed before
Jesus in dative constructions. Paul says en Christō Iēsou,
but on the contrary dia Iēsou Christou.[5]

In the use of the article it is to be observed that the
genitive tou Christou is placed after an articular noun and,
on the contrary, only Christou is used after an anarthrous
noun.[6] The article is used with the dative when it is not

38

governed by a preposition.[7] Otherwise, _Christos_ is used most frequently without an article; where the article is used it is to be explained as an anaphora. In an analogous fashion the forms _Iēsous_ and _ho Iēsous_ are also alternated.[8] However, the article with _Christos_ may, in a few cases, show that the content of the noun has not been fully lost.

Formal considerations by themselves hardly account for the variations in the mode of expression. One can also observe that Paul preferred one or another expression for specific contexts.[9] However, one should not overemphasize the significance of the particular forms of a name that are chosen at different times. This is confirmed by the frequent textual variants; only rarely do they transgress the bounds of customary Pauline usage or alter interpretation.

At this point, as at many others, the terminology of the Pastorals differs from that of the genuine letters. In the Pastorals, the form "Christ Jesus" completely dominates. From one Pauline epistle to another the different forms appear with varying frequency but no single letter exceeds the bounds established by the others. It has been assumed that _ho Christos_ is used in the sense of "the Messiah" in Ephesians (and Colossians), thus differing from the other Pauline epistles.[10] However, I have not been able to find this view confirmed by clear evidence. Even in these epistles it is never _necessary_ to understand _Christos_ as a messianic title.

Only contextual exegesis can decide to what degree the notion of the messiahship of Jesus is found in a particular passage. Generally this does not yield, I admit, an unequivocal result. But there is at least one passage, Romans 9:5, where the result is unambiguous. Anyone who knows the original meaning of the name understands that the Christ belongs to Israel, precisely as Messiah. There are other places as well where the careful reader would detect messianic connotations. In most of these cases,[11] though not in all,[12] the definite article is used with Christos. Paul speaks most clearly of the messiahship of Jesus in Romans 1:2-4, but it is still questionable if Christos is to be especially stressed in the expression, "Jesus Christ our Lord."

The result appears to be slight but it does signify something. As the matter stands, it is clear that the name Christ receives its content not through a previously-fixed conception of messiahship but rather from the person and work of Jesus Christ. An interpretatio christiana is carried out completely. Nevertheless, the name "Christ" retains a certain peculiar connotation in contrast to the true proper name, "Jesus." The name "Christ" has content: it expresses more of the nature and significance of Jesus. This is not, however, to distinguish between the person and the office. Everything that Jesus is and does, he is and does as the Christ. In Paul the name "Christ" is not a title to be detached from the person and work of Jesus Christ. As matters stand it is only natural that in individual cases one cannot clearly distinguish between statements where the name "Christ" is used only as a proper name and others where the appellative force is still felt. The only relevant question is how far and in what manner the messiahship of Jesus is expressed in all that Paul says.

Historical Setting

The historical question primarily concerns the place of Pauline usage within the framework of general early Christian usage. Within the non-Pauline works of the New Testament Christos is used as an actual title in Matthew, Mark, Luke, Acts, John, 1 John and Revelation.[13] As a part of Jesus' name, Christos is used chiefly in the form Iēsous Christos.[14] On the

other hand, only infrequently is the simple (<u>ho</u>) <u>Christos</u> used
as a designation of the person (thus 1 Peter and Hebrews).[15]
In the New Testament the sequence <u>Christos Iēsous</u> is found
almost exclusively in Paul.[16]

From this evidence several historically informative inferences can be made: Paul represented a strikingly advanced
stage in the evolution that transformed <u>Christos</u> from a messianic designation to Jesus' second proper name. Certainly this
historical development has not moved in a single straight line;
the theological content of the name could always be reactual-
ized.[17] It is quite probable that from the very earliest period many Gentile Christians understood "Christ" as a proper name
(cf. Acts 11:26) and only later were taught its significance.
One must be aware that the epistles may provide a somewhat one-
sided view of the apostle's usage. To Jews he may have spoken
in another manner (cf. Acts 17:3; 18:5; 26:23). To them the
messiahship of Jesus must have been set forth more thematical-
ly. This means that we must also reckon with the probability
that the messiahship of Jesus had for Paul himself a greater
significance than emerges directly from the usage of the name
"Christ" in his epistles.

The usage in the other New Testament writings cannot be
understood as a further development of Pauline but only of
pre-Pauline usage. This terminological independence probably
reflects christological tradition independent of Paul. This
is especially important for evaluation of the Johannine writings. The first clear case of Pauline influence upon usage
may be seen in Clement and Ignatius, especially in the formula
<u>en Christō Iēsou</u>. Paul's unemphatic use of <u>Christos</u> presup-
poses that it is part of the standard Christian vocabulary.
It is to be explained only by assuming that the confessions
and proclamation of the Aramaic-speaking church were summarized

in the affirmation: "Jesus is the Messiah." One must also
presuppose that there was a pre-Pauline, Greek-speaking church
in which "Christ" was used as a name for Jesus. His dignity
was expressed through other titles, especially kyrios.[18] Paul
already assumes the interpretatio christiana of the messianic
title Christos.

This forces us to face the question of the origin of
Pauline Christology, a topic we can treat only briefly here.
It has been asserted that Paul applied to Jesus his Jewish
messianic conceptions, setting within this framework Jesus'
earthly life as a proleptic manifestation of the transcendent
Messiah (W. Wrede, M. Brückner).[19] Studies in the history of
religions have proved that the situation is more complicated.
The terminology of Pauline Christology and its content stem
from many sources, and even terms with Old Testament and Jewish roots cannot all be derived from messianic ideology. Above
all it can hardly be doubted today that the basic elements of
Paul's Christology were already present in pre-Pauline Hellenistic Christianity.[20] The christological differences between
Palestinian and Hellenistic communities were hardly as great
as Bousset, for example, assumed. What provides the content
of the word "Christ" in Paul is less Paul's pre-Christian
messianic concept than the pre-Pauline Christology of the
church.

Perhaps at this point we may go one step farther along
the uncertain path of historical conjecture. On the road to
Damascus, Paul was convinced that the crucified Jesus was
really the Messiah. The important point is not that he applied
his conception of the Messiah to Jesus, but rather that he was
now called to proclaim the faith in Jesus the Messiah which he
had persecuted earlier. Peter and his fellow disciples probably recognized that Jesus was the Messiah before they under-

42

stood what his messiahship involved. On the contrary, Paul always understood the terms "Messiah and Christ" applied to Jesus as they were interpreted by Christians.

Nevertheless, or perhaps precisely for that reason, Paul's proclamation of Christ has a unique character. The revelation of the Son of God signified for him an abrupt break with the past. There is a correlation between this experience and his emphasis that through the cross and resurrection of Christ the old had actually passed away. Even to know Christ "according to the flesh" is to remain in the past. To be sure, for Paul the earthly Jesus is the Christ, the Son of God, born of the seed of David; but Jesus' Davidic birth and life meant not a kingly, messianic grandeur, but rather humiliation, obedience and suffering.

The resume of the gospel in Romans 1:2-4 conforms to a traditional christological pattern (cf. 2 Tim. 2:8 and further Acts 2:30-35; 13:23-37 and Mark 12:35-37). What is peculiarly Pauline is the emphatic contrast between "according to the flesh" and "according to the spirit of holiness," whereby the Davidic birth and the resurrection are related antithetically. The summary of the gospel in Romans 1:2-4 foreshadows the two great antitheses of Romans, flesh and spirit, law and Christ. The early Christian interpretation of Jesus' messiahship, which Paul took over, receives a specifically Pauline sharpening.

Theological Significance

The theological question is complicated because Jesus' messiahship is not a dogmatic element which can be isolated from Paul's total Christology. To say that Christ is "God's Son" is to say much more than "Jesus is the Messiah." Nevertheless, Jesus' divine sonship includes his messianic office.[21]

In Paul one should not even try to distinguish between a theocratic and a metaphysical understanding of "Son of God."

The lordship of Jesus expressed by the title kyrios transcends all Jewish concepts of messiahship. The preeminence of this title was favored both by the antithetical analogy to the many divine "lords" of the Oriental-Hellenistic-Roman world and by the use of kyrios by Greek-speaking Jews to render the Tetragrammaton. Probably the earthly master was addressed as "our Lord"; this same address was later used to invoke the risen Christ. Yet the significance of Psalm 110 ought not to be overlooked; to say "Jesus is Lord" implies that he is the messianic sovereign at God's right hand.[22] Kyrios is to some extent an appropriate rendering of "Messiah" because Christos had no special connotations in Greek. At this point the interpretatio graeco and the interpretatio christiana coincide.

The content of the messianic idea has been changed in many respects by the Graeco-Christian interpretation; but much has been preserved. One basic aspect of Jesus' messiahship is that he is the fulfiller of the Old Testament promises: Christ died for our sins and rose on the third day "according to the scriptures" (cf. Rom. 1:2f.; 1 Cor. 15:3f.). Paul took up the scriptural proof for Jesus' messiahship and developed it further. In the extant epistles, to be sure, we find only traces of such scriptural proof.[23] Later the messianic idea was preserved chiefly in the context of Christian interpretation of the Old Testament; often the proof of Jesus' messiahship from scripture was no longer an integral part of the dogmatic structure. In Paul, however, this is not the case; for him the messiahship of Jesus is essential for the inner coherence of his Christology.

Because Jesus is the Messiah the Christ-event is understood as an "eschatological event." The parousia of Jesus is

44

described with features taken from early Christian eschatology.[24] However, it is of more significance that Paul understands the coming of Jesus, his death, and his resurrection, as eschatological events. "In the fullness of time" God sent his Son;[25] as the "first-born from the dead" Jesus was raised.[26] Christ is the "Last Adam," the second "Man."[27] (Is this to be seen as a Graeco-Christian interpretation of the "Son of Man?") Christ died "to deliver us from the present evil age" (Gal. 1:4). Reconciliation is the eschatological counterpart to creation (Col. 1:15-20). The exaltation of Jesus is proclaimed as a heavenly, eschatological enthronement.[28]

In addition to the christological interpretation of the Old Testament and the eschatological interpretation of the Christ-event, the ecclesiology of Paul is an indirect witness to the significance of the messiahship of Jesus. Because Jesus is the Messiah, the ones who believe in him are the "saints" of the end of time, the ekklesia of God, the true children of Abraham, and therefore the "Israel of God."[29]

Even Paul's doctrine of salvation must be considered in this context. The coming, the death, the resurrection and the exaltation of Christ are accomplished events of the end of time and mark the end of the old aeon and the inauguration of the new. The doctrine of the justification of the sinner, the concept of dying and rising "with Christ" and the idea of the new being "in Christ" must be understood within this eschatological framework.[30] Jesus' messiahship is the latent presupposition for all of this.

The same applies to the Pauline doctrine that Christ is the end of the law. Faith in Christ implies for Paul that God bestowed eschatological justification and salvation through him, apart from the law. The believer is therefore justified

45

while a sinner and not as one who is just through the law.
Whoever insists on the validity of the law for the believer
does not simply err, but denies the grace of God and the effi-
cacy of Christ's death (cf. esp. Gal. 2:15-20). Only because
he has freed the sinner from the law can Christ grant him the
gift of eschatological righteousness--and only in this way can
he be the Christ. That the messiahship of Jesus stands in
contradiction to the law as the final codification of the God-
man relationship is the basic assumption common to Paul the
persecutor and Paul the apostle.

For the apostle the law is undeniably the law of God.
Only those who are redeemed by Christ and who die with him to
the law are freed from the law. Freedom from the law has as
its presupposition that Christ himself was under the law, became the "curse" and died to the law.[31] Thus it was essential
for the Pauline-Christian interpretation of Jesus' messiahship
that Christ belonged, according to the flesh, to Israel. This
is necessary not only for liberation from the law but also for
fulfilment of the promises (Rom. 15:8; cf. Gal. 3:16). For
Paul the incarnation of the Son of God is not an abstract
assumption of humanity but rather a coming "from the seed of
David," under the law (Rom. 1:3; Gal. 4:4).

Because the inseparability of Christ and Israel is
grounded in the promise of God, it is not invalidated by Israel's lack of faith. Therefore Paul says in Romans "first the
Jews." The practical corroboration of this is his collection
for and overall relation to the early apostles and the Jerusalem congregation. Paul apparently attached little importance
to teaching pagans the meaning of the name "Christ." But his
entire work as an apostle is conditioned by the messiahship of
Jesus. Paul could become the apostle to the Gentiles because
the crucified and risen Jesus was the Messiah of Israel; his

46

work as the apostle to the Gentiles aimed, in turn, at the salvation of Israel (Rom. 11:11ff.).

In the end shall "all Israel be saved"; for Jesus continues to be Israel's Messiah. For Paul the parousia is connected with Jerusalem: "From Zion shall come the deliverer; he shall banish godlessness from Jacob" (Rom. 11:26; cf. also 2 Thess. 2:4, 8). This non-spiritualized, Old Testament messianic expectation cannot be regarded as an isolated and inconsequential rudiment in the Son of God and kyrios Christology. On the contrary, it is confirmed here that Jesus' messiahship actually had a basic significance for the total structure of Paul's Christology. If Paul reckoned with a double resurrection and a messianic interregnum (cf. 1 Cor. 15:23-28), this would be another testimony to the importance of the messianic idea.[32]

According to Paul, Christ is the Lord of the church and the church is his body. It is noteworthy that the unity of Christ and the church has been emphasized in our time. This unity, however, is fatally misunderstood, if by it the church is glorified and the sovereignty of Christ is in any way impugned. Against an ecclesiastical arrogance the apostle himself has already raised a protest in Rom. 11:17ff. That Christ is and continues to be the Messiah of Israel preserves the lordship of Christ over the church and calls attention to the fact that the church of the Gentiles exists only out of the free grace of God.

THE PROBLEM OF THE HISTORICAL JESUS

The historical Jesus has become a problem for us. That does not mean that Jesus generally or primarily is a problem. Whatever the problem, we have a direct impression of Jesus as his figure encounters us in the Gospels. This is enough for the simple, believing Christian; in life and death he may set his hope on Jesus as he learns to know him through the Holy Scriptures. The problem of the historical Jesus first arises in connection with critical reflection which raises the question as to what can be ascertained about Jesus in purely historical critical fashion. The concept of the "historical Jesus," as I use it here, designates Jesus as the object of methodical, critical, historical research, and the picture of him which can be drawn by such research. It is this historical Jesus which has become a problem for us.

In the form in which it is posed today, this problem is of relatively recent date. The older Catholic and confessional Christianity was certain that the Gospels as canonical Holy Scriptures give information about Jesus which is absolutely reliable historically. The question was merely how the individual Scriptures could be brought into complete harmony with each other. For the rationalistic and liberal theology the relation between the historical Jesus and the Christ of church dogma became a problem, but for it the doctrine of the church was problematic and not the historical Jesus. Rather, it was assumed that the real picture of Jesus could be reproduced by critical historical research, and that this picture could serve as the basis for a purification and renewal of Christianity.

For present-day theology, however, it is precisely the

historical Jesus that has become a problem. A symptom of this
is that our time abounds with Jesus novels, but descriptions
of Jesus' life which raise more scientific claims are written
almost exclusively by outsiders and dilettantes. New Testament scholars know only too well how difficult the task is
and how uncertain the attempts at solution are. The leading
spirits among them content themselves with writing terse and
sketchy descriptions, in which, on the basis of their detailed
research, they emphasize the elements which they regard as
essential. It is peculiar, moreover, that the popularity of
literature on the life of Jesus appears to be on the increase
in the Catholic sector, while at the same time it has become
suspect for German Protestantism, the classic sphere of research on the life of Jesus.

The problem concerns not only the question whether it is
at all possible to give a scientifically founded and tenable
description of the life of Jesus; it also involves the question concerning the relevance of such a description for theology and the church. It is of the nature of the case that
such can only be attained by means of the usual historical
critical method, "the profane scientific method," as it is
sometimes put in theological circles. Already, however, the
methods employed prevent the recognition of what is essential
for faith; namely, that Jesus Christ is the Son of God and the
living Lord. It is understandable that the question is raised
whether or not faith, the church, and theology must keep to
that which is written in the New Testament, without troubling
with the alleged historical Jesus of critical science.

Today the uncertainty in face of such questions appears
to be very great. The following essay represents an attempt
to contribute to the clarification of the historical and the
theological problem.[1] First of all, the present state of the

problem and its presuppositions in the history of research
must be viewed somewhat more precisely.

The History of the Problem

The concept "the historical Jesus" as well as the scientific research on the life of Jesus came into being in the
period of the Enlightenment. The first presupposition for
this study was the appearance of a historical source-criticism
and the application of its methods to the Gospels, first of
all in a quite naive, rationalistic manner, then later in a
more methodical fashion. Albert Schweitzer in his Quest of
the Historical Jesus, written with the one-sidedness of genius,
has correctly pointed to a second presupposition: "When at
Chalcedon the West overcame the East, its doctrine of the
two natures dissolved the unity of the Person, and thereby
cut off the last possibility of a return to the historical
Jesus.... This dogma had first to be shattered before men
could once more go out in quest of the historical Jesus, before they could grasp the thought of His existence."[2]

Liberation from dogma could now assume various forms. A
few scholars went to work in a radical way and utilized the
"historical" description of Jesus as a means of getting free
from Christianity as such. That holds true for the pioneer of
the German Life-of-Jesus research, Hermann Samuel Reimarus.
Strongly influenced by English deists he portrays Jesus as a
political messianic pretender and his disciples as frauds.
For such radicalism, however, he found relatively few disciples
in the following century. The Life-of-Jesus research, in its
classic period of the nineteenth century, was in the main a
gigantic attempt to get free from the christological dogma of
the church, but at the same time to maintain the uniquely religious significance of Jesus. In carrying this through there

were many possible variations on the sliding scale between
strictly conservative and quite radical views. Differences
could occur in the way in which they maintained the unique
position of Jesus. Rationalism emphasized especially the
teaching of Jesus and his moral example. Later, Jesus' portrait and his God-consciousness assumed the center of the
stage. For Ferdinand Christian Baur's research, carried on
under the influence of Hegel, the decisive thing was that in
Jesus the consciousness of the unity of God and man had first
broken through. On the basis of this presupposition, the historical Jesus could now indeed become a problem; Baur himself
saw in the speculative theology of German idealism a Gnosticism of a higher order. The problem was actualized by David
Friedrich Strauss and his radical scepticism over against the
historicity of the Gospel tradition. Indeed, the solution of
the problem for Strauss was given in advance by the Hegelian
philosophy: The essential thing is the Christ idea, the idea
of God-manhood, realized in the total history of the human
race. What Jesus as a historical person was or was not was
therefore irrelevant.

The speculative theology rapidly drew to a close. The
crisis called forth by Strauss led to an even more intensive
preoccupation with the historical Jesus. Thereafter the Life-
of-Jesus research not only stood under the aegis of the strug-
gle for freedom from dogma, but also under that of the apologetic defense against Strauss. In the period of empiricism
there was also the desire to erect a secure historical basis
for Christian faith. It was assumed that the necessary basis
in the sources had been found by means of the Marcan hypothesis and the two source theory.

In contrast to rationalism and speculative theology, the
later liberal theology was more anti-metaphysical and anti-

51

intellectual. To be sure, Jesus' proclamation--e.g., of the
fatherly love of God and the infinite worth of the individual
human soul--could be strongly emphasized, but that which was
really decisive and unique was found in Jesus' personality,
his religion or his "inner life." Jesus lived in a unique
relationship of sonship to God and thus made it possible for
us as well to live in divine sonship of faith. Following
upon such an evaluation of the person of Jesus it was possible
for a "liberal-positive" mediating theology to preserve or gain
a positive relation to the apostolic proclamation of Jesus as
Savior and Lord. Liberal theology has been of influence within the Scandinavian churches chiefly in this mediating form.

In its more radical form, interest in the historical Jesus not only led to liberation from dogma, but also to a break
with the apostolic proclamation of the Christ underlying that
dogma. That came sharply to light in the debate concerning
Jesus and Paul, so intensively carried on at the turn of the
century. Paul was represented as a second founder of Christianity, who replaced the simple teaching of Jesus with his complicated doctrine of redemption. Of course, this debate in its
extreme form was quite senseless, as leading liberal theologians soon recognized; for the main features of the Pauline
preaching of Christ already existed in the church before Paul.
The real problem is not "Jesus and Paul," but rather, "Who was
Jesus and what has the church made of him?"

We would misinterpret this whole stream of research if we
were to overlook the fact that a real piety was joined to this
interest in the historical Jesus, his life, and his portrait.
But we will have to agree with Albert Schweitzer's evaluation
of the Jesus research of the nineteenth century that each
epoch in theology rediscovered its own ideas in Jesus, "otherwise it could not endow Him with life." "But it was not only

52

each epoch that found its reflection in Jesus; each individual created Him in accordance with his own character."[3] Modern religiosity not only gave rise to the quest of the historical Jesus behind and beyond the New Testament, but also to the method by which it was done. This was candidly expressed by the otherwise so critical and level-headed Adolf Jülicher in the masterpiece of his youth: "I could not understand the Lord, and thus could not love him, if a Galilean spring, sunny days with an inspired view of high mountains, had not preceded His Easter-death in Jerusalem."[4] This contrast between the bright spring in Galilee and the dark days in Jerusalem was common to all presentations in the life of Jesus.

All the liberal biographies of Jesus shared the conviction of having in the historical Jesus an ally in their efforts toward a modern theology and a broad-minded Christianity. Accordingly, the historical Jesus was modernized. This liberal Jesus-religion which wished to build on a historical Jesus freed from churchly dogma and isolated from the apostolic preaching has become an impossibility for us today. That same critical-historical research on the Bible which grew in connection with the liberal theology is responsible for it. It is to the unfading glory of this latter movement that it had the courage and the truthfulness to carry on a historical research which undermined its own dogmatic views.

The decisive blows against the liberal interpretation of the historical Jesus were already dealt at the turn of the century, though their effect only gradually became clear. The blows came from various sides. One of them struck at the sources for a presentation of the life of Jesus. In the Gospel of Mark some deletions had been made and were attributed to the theology of the church; otherwise it was thought to be a historically reliable source of the life of Jesus. However,

Wilhelm Wrede in his Das Messiasgeheimnis in den Evangelien
(1901) showed that this approach was fundamentally uncritical
and unhistorical. The oldest Gospel, according to its basic
structure, was already dogmatic, dominated by the faith in
Jesus' messianic secret. The significant thing about Wrede's
book was above all its new orientation in method. He put his
finger on the sore spot: "Scientific research on the life of
Jesus suffers from psychological conjecture."[5] A genuinely
critical and historical treatment must abandon psychological
hypotheses in order to study the extant sources in all candor,
first of all as witnesses to the faith and theology of the
evangelists and the communities in which they lived. From this
standpoint there was no longer any principal difference between
Mark and John, and in respect to the gulf which had developed
between Jesus and Paul, the Gospels now were to a certain extent removed from the historical Jesus and ranged on the side
of Paul.

Julius Wellhausen's contributions to Gospel research
moved in the same direction. As a direct result of the radi-
calizing of criticism he came to the conclusion in his
Einleitung in die drei ersten Evangelien that "without his
later influence in the community we can visualize nothing of
the religious personality of Jesus. It always appears only in
a reflection, broken by the medium of the Christian faith."[6]
In our century the form-critical school has attached itself to
Wrede and Wellhausen--although the form-critical method in itself does not need to be bound to this specific tradition of
research, as some have incorrectly supposed. It has become a
main concern of Gospel research to understand the evangelical
tradition in connection with its life situation in the church.
This function of the tradition and the interest of faith connected with it has determined the selection, formation, col-

lection, and writing of the recollected words of Jesus and episodes from his life. The theology of the church, therefore, is not only a disturbing element which appeared subsequently and falsified the genuine picture of Jesus; rather, it was there from the very beginning and explains why any recollections about Jesus were retained in the tradition.

Another blow against the leading liberal theology came from the school of the history of religions. In this school there was opposition first of all to the modernizing of primitive Christianity which is rather to be placed within the framework of Hellenistic syncretism. Significant for our problem was the fact that whereas the earlier liberal theology laid the chief emphasis on the ethical sphere, now the specifically religious was more clearly featured; for primitive Christianity the uniqueness of Jesus lay not in his religious-ethical personality, but rather in the fact that he was the Redeemer and Lord of the community, the "cult hero," as it was put. It was thereby made clear that for primitive Christianity the significance of Jesus was totally different than the evaluation placed upon him by modern Christianity.

When the need arose, radical Gospel criticism and the "religio-historical" view of primitive Christianity could still be joined to a typically liberal picture of the historical Jesus, although in that case the historical connection between Jesus and primitive Christianity threatened to break completely. The attacks were also directed against the liberal picture of Jesus itself. Within liberalism Johannes Weiss gave the storm signal. In his _Predigt Jesu vom Reiche Gottes_ he demonstrated that "the idea of the Kingdom of God in Ritschl's theology and in the preaching of Jesus are two very different things."[7] The message of Jesus was eschatological. Albert Schweitzer proceeded further on this course. For him not only

the kingdom of God in the preaching of Jesus was to be understood eschatologically; "thorough-going eschatology" offered
him the key for understanding the whole life of Jesus. The
dogmatic conception of his mission was not something added
later; Jesus himself understood his life and suffering in the
light of an eschatological dogmatic. Of course, less notice
was paid Schweitzer's own attempt at solution than his settle-
ment with the history of research "from Reimarus to Wrede."
Contrary to the author's intention, the Quest of the Historical
Jesus introduced a period of scepticism into this research.
Schweitzer could maintain that the result of the Life-of-Jesus
research was negative:

> The Jesus of Nazareth who came forward publicly as the
> Messiah, who preached the ethic of the Kingdom of God, who
> founded the Kingdom of Heaven upon earth, and died to give His
> work its final consecration, never had any existence. He is a
> figure designed by rationalism, endowed with life by liberal-
> ism, and clothed by modern theology in an historical garb.[8]

> The study of the Life of Jesus has had a curious history.
> It set out in quest of the historical Jesus, believing that
> when it had found Him it could bring Him straight into our time
> as a Teacher and Savior. It loosed the bands by which He had
> been riveted for centuries to the stony rocks of ecclesiastical
> doctrine, and rejoiced to see life and movement coming into the
> figure once more, and the historical Jesus advancing, as it
> seemed, to meet it. But He does not stay; He passes by our
> time and returns to His own.[9]

The eschatological expectation is not the only aspect
uniting Jesus with Judaism of the first century, however.
That he was part of it has also become clear in many other connections. In this area, of course, scholars of another school
have accomplished more than the liberals. The latter had generally presented Die Predigt Jesu in ihrem Gegensatz zum
Judentum (Bousset, 1892), and had drawn rather a caricature of
Pharisaism, a dark background for the portrait of Jesus' personality which shone all the brighter. The school of the history of religions was primarily interested in primitive Chris-

tianity as a syncretistic religion and emphasized the influence of oriental Hellenism. The conservative theologians showed a preference for the Jewish background in order to find a support for the historical credibility of the gospel tradition. It was hardly their intention to bring to light what was strange and ancient in the Judaism of Jesus himself.

Jewish scholars also took pains in a most profitable way to illuminate the Palestinian background of the gospel history. Influenced by Jewish emancipation and religious liberalism, they began research on the historical Jesus. The strange result was that liberal Jews could draw an ideal picture of Pharisaism strikingly reminiscent of the liberal picture of Jesus. Even in Judaism could be found faith in God as loving Father, emphasis on morality and many other things. It is not surprising that they made contact with the research on Jesus done by Christian theologians, in order to utilize it to the advantage of reformed Judaism,[10] for this historical Jesus belonged to Judaism as one of its noblest figures, though a few prejudices and exaggerations on the part of his followers could explain why he became the Founder of a new, non-Jewish religion. It also became clear to them that it was faith in Jesus as the crucified and risen Son of God which was at the heart of Christianity, and which alone differentiated it from a reformed Judaism. Wellhausen expressed the same insight briefly, tersely, and somewhat brutally: "Jesus was no Christian, he was a Jew."[11]

In its attempt to discover the essence of Christianity in the "religion of Jesus," theology, characterized by the slogan "back to the historical Jesus," had lost the historical ground beneath its feet. The lectures which Adolf von Harnack delivered on "What is Christianity?" at the turn of the century were not the program for a new era, but were rather the epi-

logue to an epoch in the history of theology which was fast
coming to a close. The dilemma into which liberal theology
had fallen was clearly seen by Wellhausen: "Without the Gospel and without Paul even Judaism would still have to cling to
Jesus.... We cannot go back to him, even if we wanted to....
For if the Gospel were removed, the historical Jesus would be
a very dubious and unsatisfactory substitute as a basis for
religion."[12] Even Wrede, so it is reported, is supposed to
have suffered from the discrepancy between the results of his
research and the piety of liberal Christianity. But these men
could not indicate a way out of the dilemma.

Albert Schweitzer found his own way. His criticism of
the modern liberal picture of Jesus not only originated in
scientific research; it was the result of a reaction to his
contemporaries who lacked the sense for the "elementary."
Philosophically and religiously he found the solution in an
ethical voluntaristic mysticism for which Jesus was not the
basis of religion, but indeed an enlivening and inspiring factor: "He comes to us as One unknown, without a name, as of
old, by the lake-side, He came to those men who knew Him not.
He speaks to us the same word: 'Follow thou me!'"[13] Obedience to this word led Schweitzer from scientific theology to
the forest of Africa. His lifework attests to the power which
can lie in a liberal Christianity, but may also raise the
question whether it can exist elsewhere than in the shadows of
a churchly Christianity. Schweitzer's intensely personal solution could not guide the further work of theology on the
problem of the historical Jesus. How many seminal insights
his conception contained were first made clear by the publication of his work The Mysticism of Paul the Apostle.

In the main, little note was first taken of the theological crisis which resulted from the work of Wrede and Wellhausen,

Weiss and Schweitzer, the school of the history of religions,
and Jewish research on Jesus. The consequences became clear
only gradually, and that is understandable. These scholars
and schools of research were in part mutually opposed, and
each of them could properly be criticized for its one-sidedness and exaggerations. Liberal theology disintegrated only
after the First World War, but more because of studies on Paul
and the Reformation than research on Jesus. This theological
reversal would not have been possible, however, if New Testament research had not undermined the liberal Jesus-religion a
few decades earlier.

Conservative theology had remained somewhat reserved over
against the Life-of-Jesus research. Hence, without concerning
itself with the crisis in this research, it could continue
working in the old way relatively undisturbed--more so in
Scandinavian countries than in Germany. To a certain extent,
these conservatives took a kind of morbid pleasure in the dis-
solution of liberal theology. For the most part, however,
they were too preoccupied with apologetics of defending the
genuineness of New Testament Scriptures and traditions to have
been able to make a decisive contribution to the critical research on the life of Jesus.

There were also theologians of a conservative temper who
combined a deep anchoring in biblical Christianity with an
openness to the questions with which scholarship had to deal.
Even before the problem of the historical Jesus had become
critical, and when the Life-of-Jesus research was still in
full bloom, Martin Kähler had written his book The So-called
Historical Jesus and the Historical Biblical Christ. In it he
pointed out a way which was to be significant for the future.
Kähler stated that the foundation of faith cannot be a scientifically reconstructed and therefore necessarily hypothetical

historical Jesus, but rather must be a Jesus Christ as proclaimed by the apostles in the preaching which established the
church. The Gospels are not sources for the biography of
Jesus, but rather are "sermons on the Messiahship of the Crucified," "passion stories with a lengthy introduction."

Upon publication Kähler's book aroused lively discussion,
but it had no decisive influence at first and could be ignored
in Schweitzer's Quest of the Historical Jesus. It had its
real effect only in our century, following the crisis in the
Life-of-Jesus research. After the First World War his ideas
were taken up and further elaborated. Once more it has become
clear to us that Christian faith relates to the Jesus of Nazareth who is preached in the apostolic proclamation as the crucified and risen Lord. That which gives the various New Testament writings their inner unity is not a theoretical dogma, nor
is it the inspiring impression of the personality of Jesus, but
rather the gospel of the act of God in Jesus Christ, in whom
forgiveness of sins, righteousness, and life are given to us.
The message of the apostles is the proclamation of a kerygma
for which they are commissioned by the appearances of the
risen Lord. The resurrection of Jesus stands at the center of
the New Testament and cannot be removed from this place without a resultant collapse. The recollections of the historical
Jesus were preserved, formed, and interpreted within the framework of the proclamation concerning the risen Lord, and for
Christian faith this interpretation is the proper and legitimate one. Only by faith in the apostolic gospel is it possible to hold fast to the unique religious significance of Jesus.
For a purely immanent, historical view he can only be unique
in that relative sense in which other great men may be called
unique. If the liberal theologians wish to hold fast to the
unique significance of the historical Jesus in another and

more absolute sense, that is an aftereffect of ecclesiastical, dogmatic Christianity.

Reducing it to a brief formula, one may say that the Life-of-Jesus theology was superseded by a kerygmatic theology. To some extent, a historical formulation of the question was now more or less consistently rejected: The extant Gospels are the only things to which we must hold fast. My honored teacher Ragnar Asting said, e.g., that the Gospels are "directed forwards," bearers of a creative proclamation; we should believe them, instead of inquiring into the historical verifiability of what is reported. He was not the only one who tended to regard the attempt to penetrate behind the Gospels to the historical Jesus as a scientifically insoluble and unfruitful task, as well as a theologically illegitimate inquiry. This new kerygmatic-theological orientation does not imply, however, that New Testament scholarship has landed in a neo-orthodoxy free of problems instead of working with serious historical questions. Just as the Life-of-Jesus theology, so also the kerygmatic theology appears in an ecclesiastically conservative as well as in a more radical form. The question for debate is not merely to what degree the old dogma of the church is a legitimate and necessary interpretation of the apostolic kerygma, but also the question, how the kerygma is to be interpreted today--the problem of demythologizing.

In spite of all its dependence on the older critical research, even Bultmann's existential interpretation must be viewed as a variant of the kerygmatic theology; it is concerned neither with the Christ idea nor with the personality of Jesus as accessible to historical research, but rather with Jesus Christ proclaimed in the gospel. The debate on demythologizing, however, has shown that we cannot so quickly dispense with the problem of the historical Jesus. Already a certain

reaction to a thoroughgoing kerygmatic theology appears to
have set in. As Ernst Käsemann has recently pointed out, an
interesting shift in fronts has come about; in reaction to
Bultmann's radicalism, an attempt is being made to counteract
a separation of kerygma from tradition.[14] In a most spirited
manner, Ethelbert Stauffer has begun to advocate a renewal of
the Life-of-Jesus research on the basis of an inquiry into the
historical context of the New Testament.[15]

It is impossible to return to the precritical evaluation
of the Gospels as historical source documents. Archaeological
discoveries and more recent researches on some questions may
have invalidated radical critical hypotheses and strengthened
trust in the tradition, but even if this should continue to a
much greater extent in the future, we will not be able to
avoid the new method of reading the Gospels primarily as witnesses of the primitive church. It is true, however, that it
would be premature to conclude from Kähler's theologically
significant and exegetically fruitful ideas that the question
concerning the historical Jesus is not to be put at all. To
be sure, faith comes from preaching and is not dependent upon
the historical critical work of New Testament professors. It
would be something quite different, however, to deny to scholars their work on historical questions or to oppose the use of
methods which in themselves are completely profane, but which
are the only ones at the disposal of the historian. That the
essence of Christianity cannot be found by a return to the
historical Jesus does not mean that it would be senseless and
improper to ask what we already know and are able to know
about Jesus in a purely historical way. The fact that the
problem is extremely difficult and its solution only approximate does not mean that we may simply abandon it. The curiosity which underlies all science will certainly lead to a con-

62

tinually new treatment of the problem. If we theologians ig-
nore this task, others will undertake it. Even if the question should be theologically irrelevant (more of this later),
we cannot call it illegitimate. The scientific ethos requires
that we do not avoid it, but rather work at it in all sincer-
ity, for God's law lies behind the scientific ethos. The historical critical concern with the problem of the historical
Jesus is at least an honorable task which is subject to the
distress and promise of every honorable profession, and certainly to the Pauline hōs mē ("as if not") as well.

The Historical Critical Problem

The fact that objectively assured results can only be
reached in an approximate way does not in itself distinguish
Jesus research from other historical science. The point is
rather that the difficulties with which all historical science
must grapple are especially perceptible in this area. All
historical work is influenced by the presuppositions of the
historian, and he himself is a child of his own time. That
becomes particularly noticeable when Jesus is made the object
of historical research, and even the historian can hardly deal
with Jesus without being involved in a positive or negative
way. It is a question whether personal involvement is not a
positive presupposition for a scholar's attaining to any kind
of historically fruitful results. To a certain degree, wish-
ful thinking and subjective errors can be eliminated by methodically scientific work, when the will to truth is present.
Scholars with different starting points co-operate and are able
mutually to correct each other. For that reason also, it is
not desirable that non-Christian scholars remain aloof from
this work. In certain respects even antipathy can be illuminating; Jewish scholars, e.g., can have a clear eye for what

is characteristic of Jesus.

Other difficulties for research on the historical Jesus
lie in the nature of the sources. We have no documentary reports and no traditions concerning Jesus by his enemies or
other contemporaries. Even the oldest extra-Christian references to Jesus appear to rest not on direct recollections, but
on encounters with Christians in Palestine or Rome. They may
suffice to corroborate the historical existence of Jesus, but
nothing more. Only on the basis of the New Testament writings
are we able to construct for ourselves a real picture of Jesus.
Of these the oldest were written about two decades after his
death, and all aim at nourishing faith in him; none of them
can be regarded as a neutral historical record. Once we recognize the nature of these sources, we will the more easily be
amazed at how much we still know of Jesus historically. A
great part of the tradition consists of brief, pregnant expressions and characteristic episodes which are easily committed
to memory. Very early, the tradition must have taken on a
relatively fixed form in a milieu where it was customary to
preserve recollections with great faithfulness. The interest
of faith in the tradition about Jesus served not only to shape,
but also to conserve the tradition; flights of fancy were confined within narrower limits than is the case, e.g., with the
legends of the apostles.

Only by methodically pure and critical work can the received traditions be made useful for a historical description
of Jesus, but thereby personal and current views concerning
what Jesus might have said or done should not be made a cri-
terion in the evaluation of the material in question. The
history of research has taught us what a dangerous source of
error this can be. If we want to avoid all subjective arbi-
trariness critical research on the Gospels becomes an extremely

64

complicated work requiring the highest degree of precision. The extant Gospels are first of all to be studied and interpreted as literary wholes. Their relationship to each other must be accurately examined, but even the relatively certain results of source criticism have only limited value for the historical question, for we must reckon with the fact that the oral tradition still existed in addition to and following the first written records. The possibility exists throughout that an older variant of the tradition may have been preserved in a secondary literary source.[16]

In addition to the literary investigation of the Gospels we must consider the traditio-historical study of the small or smallest units of the tradition. In addition to the Gospels, material from later sources--e.g., quotations from the church fathers, textual variants, and fragments of apocryphal gospels-- has a significance which cannot be ignored. The new material which such sources offer is extremely small and of dubious value, but the subsequent history of the gospel tradition is illuminated, and from it the cautious scholar will be able to draw a few conclusions regarding its earlier history. In further research, critical questions concerning the form, language, and substance are also to be observed. No single road leads to the goal; in spite of the very fruitful beginning of form criticism, the result has been, e.g., that the study of form has not yielded objective criteria for separating older from later traditions to the degree expected. The linguistic criteria, in their turn, lead with great probability to old traditions where the original Semitic tongue shines through but do not allow any positive decision regarding the _ipsissima_ _verba_ of Jesus. Preference for one certain method should be regarded as a calamity and, where possible, be replaced by the co-operation of a variety of specialists.

On the basis of numerous individual observations, a more comprehensive picture of the history of the tradition can then be outlined. Certain statistical, not absolute, laws and regularities emerge which leave their imprint on the formation and transformation of the tradition. It is well known that the individual sayings and narratives as such have been relatively faithfully preserved, while the evangelists and the narrators before them were much freer in the collection and arrangement of the material. Within the individual sections of the tradition greater freedom is exercised with respect to rendering introductory and concluding data than with regard to the central point. Among the different variants agreement is greatest in the rendering of the words of Jesus, but the words have not been preserved because of any reverence for the antiquarian, but because they are words of the Lord to his community. Loosed from their original situation, the words have been used and construed in a new way, a factor which has affected not only their arrangement, but also their formation. That can be most easily observed in the case of the parables.[17]

The goal of critical Gospel research is to make clear the history of the tradition about Jesus within the church. With some certainty, moreover, distinction can be made between the core of the tradition and its later elaboration. It is much more difficult to find objective criteria which can determine whether the core of a tradition is authentic or secondary. It is theoretically possible that migrant sayings have been transferred to Jesus, that words of Jewish wisdom or utterances of primitive Christian prophets have been put in the mouth of the historical Jesus, et cetera, but only very seldom can positive proof be adduced that such is really the case. Here, generally, the total perspective of the scholar is decisive for an evaluation of the case in point, and not vice versa. That can

66

easily be observed in Bultmann's History of the Synoptic Tradition, but also applies to scholars who, like myself, are inclined to believe that on the whole the church did not produce the traditions about Jesus, but rather reproduced them in a new form.

In no case can any distinct and sharp separation be achieved between genuine words of Jesus and constructions of the community. We do not escape the fact that we know Jesus only as the disciples remembered him. Whoever thinks that the disciples completely misunderstood their Master or even consciously falsified his picture may give his phantasy free reign. From a purely scientific point of view, however, it is more logical to assume that the Master is to be recognized from the circle of his disciples and its historical influence. But then it is also possible to work methodically when an attempt is made to advance from the analysis of the Gospel tradition to the description of the historical Jesus.

Even without a clear differentiation between pure history and later theology the gospel tradition permits us to draw a very clear picture of what was typical and characteristic of Jesus. Cross sections of the tradition bring to the fore what was characteristic, e.g., of his proclamation of the kingdom of God, of his position toward the law, or of his attitude toward various groups of men. Words and reports of differing form and genre, transmitted within various layers of the tradition, mutually illumine each other and yield a total picture in which there appears something that is characteristic of Jesus. Whether the historicity of individual words or episodes remains uncertain is consequently of lesser importance. The fact that the word or occurrence found a place within the tradition about Jesus indicates that it agreed with the total picture as it existed within the circle of the disciples.[18]

The cross-section method must be supplemented by drawing longitudinal lines leading from Judaism beyond Jesus to primitive Christianity. While the time when Zarathustra and Moses lived has long been the subject of debate, we know that Jesus was crucified under Pontius Pilate. The fixed starting point of all our knowledge about him is that he is the crucified one whom the community, originating in his band of disciples, believed to be the risen Messiah. We also know that Jesus worked in Israel and that he himself was born and raised a Jew, was "born of woman, born under the law." The historical Jesus is to be found at the crossroad where Christianity and Judaism begin separating from each other, although it only became gradually clear that the paths parted in such a way that Christianity appeared as a new religion alongside Judaism.

From the oldest Christian sources we must work our way backwards in the direction of Jesus. It is of great advantage that the most important groups of New Testament writings are independent of each other; Paul, the Synoptists, John, the Epistle to the Hebrews, et cetera, cannot be arranged into one straight line of development. Rather, each in its own way reflects the impression made by Jesus and the events connected with his name. Between the historical Jesus and the New Testament writings there are, of course, the Easter occurrences, but that does not alter the fact that the historian who works backwards from the various formulations of primitive Christianity toward the common starting point by this method also approaches the historical Jesus. The investigation of the tradition lying behind the Gospels is the most important, but not the only part of this work.

On the other hand, we must view Jesus within the context of Palestinian Judaism. Everything which enlarges our knowledge of this environment of Jesus indirectly extends our

knowledge of the historical Jesus himself. Since the results
in this area are relatively certain, it is a very real question whether or not the insights gained here in the long run
involve the greatest enrichment of our historical knowledge
about Jesus. Only by saving the honor of the Pharisees, e.g.,
has the unheard-of radicality of Jesus' words against the
Pharisees really come to light. It is still not possible to
estimate what the textual findings from the Qumran caves may
yield; in any case they impel us to resume the quest of the
historical Jesus. As never before we have the possibility of
tracing the trends and ideas which, both positively and negatively, form the presuppositions for his ministry.

When, on the one hand, the historian works backwards in
this way from oldest Christianity to Jesus and, on the other,
attempts to clarify the presuppositions of his appearance on
the basis of Jewish sources, quite a clear picture can be
gained of the setting into which Jesus appeared and of the
changes which his ministry effected. By this method it is
also possible to insert the transmitted words and episodes
into their original historical situation. Thus we can form an
idea of what Jesus wanted to say to the Jews of his own time
and can attempt to construct a historical picture of him.

The historian's attempt to reconstruct the historical
Jesus by the historical critical method may be compared with
the work of the archaeologist who attempts to restore an old
monument of which only the foundation and a few scattered
stones remain. He may try to draw sketches on paper in order
to show how the structure probably looked. No one will deny
him that, and it can be useful and necessary for his work. He
misleads his readers, however, when he publishes his sketch
without calling attention to the place where exact knowledge
leaves off, where he has good grounds for his reconstruction,

and where he has drawn free hand. When he finds the precise spot where one or a few of the scattered stones originally lay, it means more in the long run than such reconstructive attempts. Similarly, it is permissible to write a description of the historical Jesus, but hypotheses may not be advanced as exact scientific results. If there is an element of genius in the hypotheses, as e.g., in Albert Schweitzer's case, then they may give important impulse to further research. But over an extended period an expansion of our exact knowledge of primitive Christianity and of Judaism in Jesus' time means more for our historical knowledge of Jesus than many books about his life.

Historical studies can only approximately achieve exact results. This does not merely apply to the Jesus research, but the general truth is most particularly to be observed in the Jesus research with its involved problematic. Whoever has to fix an uncertain chronological datum, e.g., the year of the origin of a work, is only seldom in the position of finding new arguments which allow him to make a completely accurate decision. He must begin by establishing the termini a quo and ante quem and, on the basis of these two limits, try to approach the precise point of time. Even the more involved historical problems will, mutatis mutandis, have to be dealt with in a similar way. So far as Jesus is concerned, the scholar must search, on the one hand, for what can be established in any event and cannot reasonably be called into question however great the historical scepticism. Radical criticism has a necessary function here. The rule here is that it is not the nongenuineness, but contrariwise the genuineness of the indivual piece which is to be demonstrated and that a genuine transmission concerning Jesus is established only when the "tradition, for various reasons, can be neither derived from

Judaism nor attributed to primitive Christianity."[19] This
radical criticism and its results may not be dogmatized, but
must rather be regarded as one necessary heuristic principle
among others. Whatever is discovered in this way is only a
critically assured minimum.

On the other hand, the total tradition concerning Jesus
must be taken into consideration. In its totality it is theology of the church, but at the same time it is also in its
totality a reflex of Jesus' activity--a maximum which contains
everything of importance for our historical knowledge about
Jesus. To delineate this maximum more precisely is a problem
for the solution of which Stauffer's "iron rule" applies: In
dubiis pro tradito.[20] The further task consists in narrowing
the gap between the maximum of the tradition and the critically
assured minimum to the highest degree possible, in order step
by step to approach more closely to the historical Jesus. The
chief reason why the older Life-of-Jesus research became sterile and scientifically unfruitful might have been that it set out
too directly and rashly toward its goal. If today we face a
renewal of interest in Jesus research, we will have to be on
our guard against committing the same error again.

Although we are still far removed from the desired degree
of exactitude, we may construct a reasonably clear picture of
the manner of Jesus' appearance as well as of the content of
his proclamation and his teaching, and of the impression which
he made on the adherents and opponents among his contemporaries.
The sources do not permit us to say much regarding his inner
life, since they were not interested in it. The open question
is whether we may detect only characteristic features or whether it is possible to give a scientific description of the life
of Jesus founded on objective arguments. That a biography of
Jesus cannot be written is a truism today. We cannot even

write the history of Jesus' development within the period of his public ministry. The contrast between the Galilean spring and the subsequent period of defection and opposition is not sufficiently attested to in the sources, as Albert Schweitzer correctly emphasized. But Schweitzer's own theory, which did not proceed from the beginning but rather from the climax of Jesus' public life and which found the key for understanding the history of Jesus in the delay of the parousia at the time the seventy were sent out (Matt. 10:23), rested on an entirely arbitrary combination of the sources.

The difficulty of the task does not mean, however, that it would be senseless to work at it scientifically. There is a point in the life of Jesus which is unconditionally established. That is his death. A historically tenable description of the life of Jesus would only be possible in the form of a description of his death, its historical presuppositions, and the events preceding and following it. In other areas it has proved a fruitful method to begin with a very definite event and from it throw light on the preceding and following periods. In our case this could be the only practicable way because of the nature of the sources. Kähler's statement, "passion stories with a lengthy introduction," is important not only for the proper interpretation of the Gospels, but also for their use as historical sources on the life of Jesus. Historical considerations of a more general character point in the same direction. In the historical development which led to the rise of Christianity, the death of Jesus is the axis on which everything turns. "Without his death he would not have become historical at all," said Wellhausen.[21] Historical research must begin with the death of Jesus if it will inquire not only into the preaching but also into the life of Jesus.

Of course, a historical description of the death of Jesus

72

is still a most difficult and complicated task. No doubt the
Gospel reports at this point, and only at this point, are
somewhat detailed and coherent and to a certain degree are
chronologically arranged. The interest of the evangelists,
however, lies in describing Jesus' death as saving event and
as the basis of the new covenant, and not in presenting it as
a world historical phenomenon with certain historical causes
and effects. Before written Gospels existed, the oldest passion narratives which Christians read were such Old Testament
texts as Psalm 22, a practice which can often be traced in the
Gospel accounts. One must be extremely cautious about employ-
ing them in the service of historical reconstruction.

In other respects, also, our historical knowledge is extremely limited. The debate over the Sanhedrin's authority to
levy the death sentence, a debate which still has not been finally settled, provides one example. It is further questionable how much of rabbinic penal law can be traced back to the
time of Jesus. Even where that is possible, the gain is dubious, for we must reckon with the possibility that the trial of
Jesus was conducted according to the rules of presumably Sad-
ducean legal practice--if, indeed, there was any intention of
conducting before the Sanhedrin a trial against Jesus according to regular juridical forms, which is equally uncertain.
The motives which induced the Jewish authorities and Pilate to
proceed against Jesus are very difficult for us to detect.
Despite the existing difficulties, however, the attempt should
be made to begin with the death of Jesus and, with all the
available means of historical science, to study the remaining
problems of Jesus' life. There will always be much that remains doubtful, but we may be confident that research which
works energetically in this direction will attain to signifi-
cantly surer results than the previous Life-of-Jesus litera-

ture.

In any case it is clear that what we know with certainty about the life of Jesus is that it ended on the cross. That must also be kept in mind in the attempt to understand the preaching and teaching of Jesus. An obvious weakness of many descriptions of Jesus as a very pious and very humane, but somewhat harmless teacher lies in the fact that it is not understood why high priests and Romans had any kind of interest in the execution of this man. The end of Jesus' life helps to sharpen our view of the challenging claim to authority manifest in his appearance and also evident in the Sermon on the Mount. We must observe the same in the exposition of the parables; in many instances the real meaning becomes clear only when we keep in mind how, in veiled form, they express the decisive meaning Jesus attributed to his own mission.[22] Accordingly, no one can maintain that historical research has access only to the preaching of Jesus and not to his life. Rather, we must state that a historical understanding of his preaching can be attained only when it is seen in connection with his life, namely with the life which ended on the cross.

The Theological Problem

In spite of all the problems and difficulties, the inquiry into the historical Jesus is a legitimate and a fruitful task. The more difficult question is whether this work is also of significance for faith, for the church and theology. The problem becomes clear at this point when we presuppose hypothetically that it would be possible to give a scientifically founded description of Jesus' life in the form of a presentation of his death and the events preceding it. The goal would be to reach such a degree of scientific objectivity that everyone, regardless of his presuppositions of faith, would have to

74

admit that everything happened in just this way and no other. Not only the external course of Jesus' life would be illuminated, but also a series of factors influencing it. The nature and content of Jesus' preaching would also come into consideration as important elements which unleashed the opposition to him. With good reason, I assume it can be considered probable that Jesus not only foresaw his own death, but actually ascribed to it a vicarious significance and saw in it a necessary presupposition for the coming of the kingdom of God if not his own enthronement as Son of Man. For the historian, such ideas of Jesus would come into consideration as one factor among others illuminating the course of Jesus' life. Then it would be understandable why Jesus did nothing to avoid the threatening danger, but through his purification of the temple seems to have provoked the intervention of the high priests.

It is obvious that the Christian faith and the church would have only a very limited interest in such a presentation of what actually occurred, even if it could be given with a very high degree of historical probability. What alone is decisive for faith and the church, namely, that Jesus' death was a dying _for us_, would not appear at all in such a historical description of the causes and effects of his death. The historian _qua_ historian can say nothing concerning what really took place in that which occurred here--that God showed his love to us, that while we were still sinners, Christ died for us. The believing community could therefore tranquilly disregard the historical description of Jesus' death and his previous life for the sake of holding to the Gospels and to the rest of the New Testament writings. Once more it would be clear to the church that only the resurrection of Jesus from the dead and the witness of the Holy Spirit through the apostles disclose the meaning and the significance of Jesus' death

75

and his previous life. It will therefore firmly maintain that
in the New Testament and nowhere else is it revealed who Jesus
really was--without being required to contest the results of
historical science.

Faith is concerned neither with the immanent effects of
Jesus' death nor with an evaluation of his personality. Jesus'
life and death have their significance in and with the message
that God raised him from the dead. But in contrast to the
life and death of Jesus his resurrection cannot be made an
object of historical research. Only the Easter faith of the
disciples is accessible to the historian, the origin of which
he can illumine only to a certain degree. Good reasons can be
advanced for the fact that the tradition of the empty grave is
historical in essence, as von Campenhausen has recently shown.[23]

Even though it were proved beyond every doubt, however,
the historian would still find only an empty grave and no
risen Savior. The possibility of some kind of a misunderstanding or an inexplicable accident would remain. Similarly, the
revelations of the risen Lord to Peter and to the disciples
can be explained as visions and hallucinations, and even if it
could be proved that no psychological explanation suffices,
the possibility of a parapsychological interpretation remains,
and we would not be one step nearer the Christian faith, which
praises God for the fact that he has begotten us again to a
living hope through the resurrection of Jesus Christ from the
dead.

Whoever knows what historical research is and what the
resurrection of Jesus from the dead means cannot suppose that
he is able to prove the resurrection by historical arguments.
That Jesus of Nazareth is the Son of God who died for us and
rose from the dead is visible only to him who believes in him.
Objective, historically scientific arguments do not decide

concerning belief and unbelief, but rather only the personal relation to the apostolic message of the crucified and risen one, the Son of God, our Lord. Faith arises from the grace that is given us to believe in this gospel. The emphasis of kerygmatic theology that faith comes through preaching and that it is relatively uninterested in a historical Jesus research may not merely be regarded as an escape from an acute crisis in the Life-of-Jesus research, but actually rests upon a proper knowledge of what the Christian faith is.

That faith is relatively uninterested in the historical Jesus research does not mean that it is absolutely uninterested in it. To draw this conclusion would be a kerygmatic theological Docetism, or even a denial of faith in God as Creator, under whose worldly rule even the historian does his service as a scholar. The fact that Jesus can be made an object of historical critical research is given with the incarnation and cannot be denied by faith, if the latter is to remain true to itself.

The Jesus research, with its more or less debatable results has, at all events, made it clear that Jesus was really a true man with human individuality, belonging to a definite time and a definite milieu. The message of the New Testament that this man is the Son of God, the Word become flesh, can neither be proved nor refuted by the Jesus research. One thing has become clear, however: incarnation signifies not only the assumption of an abstract human nature by the godhead, but that the Word really became flesh, concrete, human history. By making this clearer, historical research has contributed toward clarifying the offence of the Christian message and the possibility of its scandal. In this way the Jesus research can occasion offences and inner conflicts from which many difficulties for Christianity have arisen and may still arise. But this has

77

not made it more difficult to have a living faith--at all events not more difficult than in the first period of the church when there was still an immediate remembrance of Jesus as a man among men and when the foolishness and the offence of the cross were not yet tempered by a traditional symbolism. The possibility of offence was not less for the contemporaries of Jesus than for us who today can make him an object of historical research. By having made this clear, historical research can help us to hear the word of the Master with new joy: "Blessed is he who takes no offence in me." Whoever in anxiety over Christianity wishes to keep critical-historical research away from Jesus should ask himself whether or not he in reality is seeking to avoid the possibility of the offence and the inner conflict in which faith must now live in the world.

In any case, the Life-of-Jesus research has this negative relevance, that it uncovers the possibility of the offence. The question is whether it has or at least can have positive significance. A tendency towards a negative answer can be observed not only in such representatives of kerygmatic theology who would hold simply to the canonical Gospels, but also in a radical critic such as Bultmann. In the case of the existentialist interpretation of the New Testament, it is only of consequence that Jesus lived and died on the cross and that this is proclaimed as the saving event to be grasped in the obedience of faith. Faith as an existential attitude is not supposed to be interested in the question of the _how_ of Jesus' life. The understanding of faith may not be interpreted as an objectifiable knowledge of whether the things to be regarded as true are dogmatic mythologoumena or are demonstrable historical facts.

In this form, therefore, the kerygmatic theology does not lead to indifference over against the historical critical

78

question, but, on the contrary, to the fact that a radical historical criticism is pressed into the service of a definite
theological conception. Criticism itself receives a theological function since it serves to make clear that faith cannot
hold to a historically unequivocal picture of Jesus' personality and that a "messianic consciousness" cannot be demonstrated as an observable phenomenon.[24] Faith has no historical security, but only the assurance given by the word of
preaching. The Gospel of John is for Bultmann the chief Gospel, not although he regards it as completely unhistorical,
but precisely because he does so. In it Jesus is described
"not as a reliably attested person in the past, but in such a
way as he is always present in the word which proclaims him
in the power of the Spirit."[25] In such a way the significance
of Jesus becomes clear for faith.

It is important to understand that historically mediated
knowledge can create no security for faith and that, converse-
ly, much that is unhistorical may be in the Gospels without
the need for faith to feel itself seriously endangered. The
existentialist interpretation carried out consistently signifies, as I have pointed out elsewhere, not only a demythologizing, but also a dehistoricizing of the New Testament.[26]
This dehistoricizing of the New Testament is an ultra-Pauline
extreme conditioned by existentialist philosophy which does
not do justice to the Gospels. Though it may be true that the
Gospels are proclamation and witness, still it would be contrary to the intention of the evangelists to declare as irrelevant the inquiry into the historicity of the narratives. In
all philosophical naivete it may be regarded as natural and
normal that even the present-day believer shares the interest
of the evangelists in preserving reliable information concerning what the Lord and Savior did at the time of his earthly

79

life and how his life took shape. This interest may lead to error, for example, when the history of Jesus is interpreted by means of improper historical categories or when a false and illusory security is sought. As a warning against this possible error, the Pauline refusal to know Christ after the flesh retains its abiding justification, but the necessity of this critical corrective does not mean that positive interest in the history of Jesus is objectionable per se. Even without seeking a false historical security, the Christian may rejoice when historical research not only brings inner conflicts for faith but shows that the historically demonstrable facts of Jesus' life are not unambiguous proofs, but are indeed visible signs to faith that Jesus was the one the New Testament proclaims him to be. When the how of the life of Jesus is declared to be theologically irrelevant, the incarnation of the Word threatens to become a paradox devoid of content. We must raise the question whether or not the dehistoricizing existentialist interpretation leads to an avoidance of the possibility of offence lying in the concrete history of Jesus and thus fails to see his hidden glory.

To require that the Jesus research should establish the glory of Jesus, conceived this way or that and established by means of objective arguments, would be the demand for a sign on the part of an unbelieving generation. On the other hand, we must openly admit that it would be fatal theologically if the result of this research would be the establishment of an irreconcilable opposition between the historical Jesus and the witness of the New Testament to Christ. Even Bultmann cannot avoid it; theologically he is not so uninterested in the question concerning the historical Jesus as might perhaps appear from some of his statements. That Jesus' preaching must be interpreted as a call to decision and in such a way that his

80

own person as bearer of the Word signifies the demand for decision[27] is rather a materially necessary presupposition for
Bultmann's interpretation of the New Testament. It follows
from this that after his death the preaching of Jesus could
only be taken up in the form of a message concerning the saving deed of God in Jesus Christ calling to decision, and not
in the form of a literal reproduction of his sayings or of a
biographical description of his life.[28]

Bultmann calls attention to the fact that the Jesus research is theologically questionable and dangerous when it
results in interpreting the historical Jesus in categories
which originate elsewhere and which are not appropriate to
him--for example, when he is presented as a teacher of timeless ideas, as a personality or as a charismatic miracle work-
er or a religious hero. The use of such categories is conditioned by the respective presuppositions of the scholar, however, and is not a necessary result of historical inquiry; its
inappropriateness is proved by the continuing research itself.

It is pertinent to ask now whether, in view of the historical sources, it is permissible to describe the historical
Jesus merely as the bearer of the Word which calls for decision. It must be the object of historical research to eliminate, as far as possible, all modern categories in order to
ascertain how Jesus was understood by his contemporaries and
how he himself wanted to be understood. It will best serve
theology and the church when it limits itself to this task
with complete impartiality. (The historian only has access to
an interpreted history of Jesus, not to the nudum factum of
the Verbum Dei incarnatum, which Stauffer supposes he is able
to illuminate by a research into the historical context of the
New Testament.)

Even a scholar who does not share Bultmann's existentialist interpretation will agree with him that the relationship between the historical Jesus and the preaching of his apostles is not a problem which threatens theology to the extent it appeared at the turn of the century. At first it appeared that the radical Gospel criticism and the history-of-religions school would lead to the assumption of an unbridgeable gulf between Jesus and the church; in this situation it is quite understandable why outsiders proceeded to deny the historical existence of Jesus. Theologically, the most important result of Albert Schweitzer's grand conception was that it pointed a way out of this dilemma: The eschatological message and the eschatological expectation bind Jesus and primitive Christianity into a unity.[29] Jesus proclaimed the nearness of the kingdom of God; indeed, as we express it today, in our correction of "thoroughgoing eschatology," he preached that in and with his own mission, his word and work, God's kingdom was already breaking in. The primitive community and Paul share the same expectation, but their place in the eschatological history of salvation is different. Neither a proof of the difference between Jesus' preaching and the teaching of his apostles from the standpoint of the history of ideas nor a proof of their connection from the standpoint of the history of their development can really lead us anywhere.

On the basis of the presuppositions common to Jesus and the primitive church, it is impossible that after the death of Jesus the disciples could have preached the message of salvation in the same form in which he himself preached it. Between Jesus and the primitive community there lie his death and resurrection as decisive events: Jesus is appointed to the position of messianic ruler in which he shall some day be revealed; those who call upon his name now already assemble themselves as the ekklesia of God in the new time of salvation. Jesus

82

research thus leads us to this alternative: Either the events of Easter and Pentecost are the preliminary fulfillment of Jesus' eschatological promise, or this promise, at the heart of his message, remained unfulfilled. Then in spite of all the inspiring impressions emanating from him, we would have to classify him among the messianic pretenders of Judaism.

Accordingly, we might say that instead of isolating the historical Jesus from the apostolic gospel and the church, the critical test of historical research has enabled us to see them in their unity. The question today is whether we may proceed still further and establish a direct connection in the sense that the historical Jesus himself intended the church. A whole series of investigations has shown what a great role church, worship, sacraments, etc., have played in primitive Christianity. There has also been the attempt to show that all this must have been rooted in the earthly life of Jesus. In the more recent Swedish theology, but not only there, much was accomplished in this direction in the last decades. Anton Fridrichsen has pointedly remarked: "Everything that Jesus does and says points toward that goal, His ecclesia."[30] With such an emphasis, the kerygmatic theology takes on the form of a new ecclesiology in which the neglect of the historical Jesus on the one hand and its positive interest in referring the church with its Christology and its sacraments back to this historical Jesus on the other seem to contradict each other.

To what degree this view of the church may correctly appeal to the results of New Testament research is still debatable on many points. The methodological difficulties are very noticeable here. Wherever we see in the Gospels a direct agreement with the Christology and the community life of the primitive church, the critical question arises as to whether or not such ideas were only subsequently dated back into Jesus' earthly life. On the other hand, the christological interpretation of the resurrection appearances and the subsequent formation of the church can hardly be understood if the words of Jesus had not already paved the way for both the Christology and the ecclesiology of the primitive church. Therefore, in such questions it is extremely difficult to attain negatively or positively to any objectively certain results; the classic example of this is the ever-fluctuating debate concerning the word of Jesus to Peter in Matthew 16. In other instances, such as the choosing and sending out of the twelve or the words of the Lord's Supper, we may assume with a greater degree of certainty that the words concerned go back to Jesus himself. As far as Christology is concerned, not only the post-Easter proclamation of the disciples, but also the fact of Jesus' crucifixion proves how easy it was to assume that he himself intended to be the Messiah even though he did not proclaim himself publicly as such. The consciousness of authority inherent in his preaching and his total attitude over against the Jewish authorities and persons points in the same direction.

It would be unnatural if the church did not have an interest in what can be rendered probable on this issue, but historical research never proceeds beyond probability. That which is to be unconditionally affirmed is that the certainty of faith rests upon the proclaimed gospel and not upon what science does or does not have to say concerning Jesus' messianic self-consciousness. Likewise, our certainty of belonging to the church of God is connected with the fact that by his death Jesus gained a people for God's own possession, and not with the fact that present-day research can advance good arguments for the idea that the ministry of the historical Jesus had the formation of a church as its goal.

The "new ecclesiology" has avoided a danger which threatens other forms of kerygmatic theology--namely, the danger of disengaging the gospel from real history, the danger of the kerygmatic-theological Docetism. In place of it another danger threatens. It would not only be scientifically but also theologically suspect if the interest in the historical Jesus should limit itself exclusively or even primarily to rendering it probable that Jesus' own work aimed at his ekklesia. It is essentially correct when Fridrichsen asserts that the unity of the New Testament can only be affirmed when Jesus is seen in his unity with the church and not in categories of personalistic idealism.[31] The danger in such a formulation lies in the fact that this unity between Jesus and the church can be understood as a kind of identity by which Jesus Christ is dissolved into the church, into its proclamation and dogma, its cultus and office.

Thus it is also a theological necessity to keep the question concerning the historical Jesus open and living, not least for the reason that the independence of Jesus over against the church must be maintained. Jesus is already in existence before and outside the proclamation of the church; he may neither be absorbed by the existential here and now of the kerygma nor by the tradition and the church. This independence of Jesus is not to be understood as an isolation, as was the case with the "back to Jesus" slogan. It does mean, however, that Jesus is present not only in the church and its proclamation, but also--and that is the first and basic thing--that he stands over against the church in sovereign freedom. Research on the historical Jesus must continually refer to this independence. It must do so primarily and simply by recalling the basic historical fact that Jesus was a Jew, "sprung from the seed of David according to the flesh." Through Jesus the church is

bound to the Scriptures of the Old Testament and to the sacred
history of Israel. That the church is the legitimate succes-
sor of the people of God of the old covenant cannot, however,
be proved with historical exactitude. The people of Israel
continued to exist alongside the church in the midst of many
sufferings which were often inflicted upon them by the believers
in Christ, but Christ is an Israelite according to the flesh,
and research on the historical Jesus makes this explicitly
clear to us. For the church this fact signifies a continual
warning against ecclesiastical self-sufficiency and self-con-
fidence. Paul was aware of this (Rom. 11), but the church
after him has only too often forgotten it.

Not only the fact that Jesus belonged to Israel but also
the nature of his historical influence within Israel constitutes a warning against that form of self-contented ecclesiasticism. The preaching and the appearance of Jesus attest to
his deep unity and solidarity with his people, the people of
God. In this solidarity, however, he appears as a man whose
word and work are a judgment upon all Jewish ecclesiasticism;
temple worship, scriptural erudition, pious practice, the
basic attitude of those who trust in the privileges of the
people of God--nothing of all that is spared. This Jesus who
chastens and reprimands the people of God is the Lord of the
church in whom we believe. This is made unmistakably clear by
research on the historical Jesus and has certain necessary
consequences, namely, that even the church of the new people
of God stands under his judgment and under the reprimand which
proceeds from him, the living Lord, who is none other than he
who once lived in Israel, the historical Jesus. When the
church is unconcerned about the historical Jesus, this will
only too easily lead to its ignoring his warning against all
ecclesiastical self-sufficiency. Already in the case of the

evangelists, and especially in Matthew, we can observe how Jesus' warning words of judgment to the Jews have received a new addressee and serve as a warning to the members of the new community (cf., e.g., 7:22f. as over against Luke 13:25ff.).[32]

To be on principle indifferent to the concrete, earthly history of Jesus might further involve the danger that the kerygma is not related to the concrete, everyday life of man, but is validated only in the abstraction of an understanding of existence or only within the sacred realm of the church. The preacher stands basically in the same post-Easter situation as the evangelists and is bound to the interpretation of the history of Jesus by the apostolic proclamation transmitted in the New Testament, but he must be allowed to go back to the alleged original meaning of a word in order, analogous with the procedure of the evangelists, to proclaim it, in view of the post-Easter situation and the change of audience, as a word of the Lord to the community of his time. Because of the special authority already ascribed to the words of the Lord in the New Testament, we cannot regard the question concerning the historical genuineness or nongenuineness of a word as completely irrelevant for theology.[33] Yet, for preaching and dogmatic reflection this question really becomes actual only in the cases when there is no real agreement of a word with the central kerygma; then we will more easily be able to disregard the word when objective historical criteria suggest that there is no authentic word of Jesus.

We have not given a dogmatic answer to the question of the theological relevance of Jesus research but have only stated a few viewpoints and random observations. I think that this must be the case if it is true that scientific research on the historical Jesus can neither be of fundamental significance for faith and the church nor can it be totally irrele-

vant. Neither the historical critical nor the theological
problem of the historical Jesus is to be answered definitively,
so that we could ever dispense with it. This problem signifies
an element of unrest for the church, but this unrest is salu-
tary and should remind us that Jesus is Lord of the church and
that the church may not make itself lord over Jesus. To the
question: Who was Jesus? the church answers with its praising
confession. It will not go astray because of the alleged
results of the Life-of-Jesus research. It would not, however,
be fidelity to its confession but rather pride if it were to
declare itself on principle uninterested in the work of a
sober historical research.

For a while it can be of benefit to New Testament research
to leave behind the attempts at historical reconstruction in
order to work at other tasks, where there are greater possi-
bilities of attaining to fruitful and certain results. But we
cannot on principle or for any length of time pass by the problem of the historical Jesus. Even the scholar who stands within the church and who would serve the church by his work cannot allow himself to be ordered by ecclesiastical courts regarding the results he must attain. Indeed, the New Testament
scholar will be interested in a co-operative effort with his
colleagues in systematic theology, because they can make clear
to him whether, with the historical methods necessary for his
work, he has also appropriated a definite historical and ideo-
logical tradition which is not appropriate to the object of
his investigations. We should neither expect nor desire that
the church's preaching and dogmatic reflection be built on the
uncertain ground of research on the historical Jesus. On the
other hand, we should retain an openness and truthfulness toward this research. We must expect of dogmatic work in Christology that it not avoid the problem of the historical Jesus,

but have a concern for a better solution than the historical
Life-of-Jesus theology and the dehistoricizing kerygmatic
theology.

RUDOLF BULTMANN'S THEOLOGY OF THE NEW TESTAMENT

The Importance of the Book

For two reasons, the appearance of Bultmann's Theology of
the New Testament[1] is a major event in the history of biblical
scholarship--(a) Bultmann is the first to publish a comprehensive treatment of New Testament theology in more than a generation. It is distinguished as much by unity of conception as
by mastery of materials. Until now, no New Testament theology
by a scholar of our generation has been equal to the standard
works of the liberal and conservative schools. Büchsel wrote
a textbook useful for the beginner. Stauffer is as arbitrary
as he is provocative. F. C. Grant has published a fine introduction to New Testament thought. The late Maurice Goguel's
two volumes on the rise of Christianity and of the church syn-
thesize the results of decades of comprehensive and penetrating study. But only Bultmann has presented a New Testament
theology of great scope in our generation.[2]

(b) It is equally important that this theology of the New
Testament is the work of Rudolf Bultmann; it is the culmination
of his lifelong work as an interpreter of the New Testament.
One might say that all his work since World War I has pointed
toward such a comprehensive summary. This book is the equal
of his two classic works, the History of the Synoptic Tradition
and his commentary on the Fourth Gospel (The Gospel of John,
ET 1971). This should be a sufficient indication of the book's
importance.

Its Place in the History of Biblical Scholarship

At the outset, it may be useful to clarify the work's
place in the history of biblical studies (cf. Epilogue II, 237-

51). It synthesizes many diverse trends in New Testament
scholarship. First of all, it is continuous with previous
work in biblical criticism and history of religions research
(II, 250). This may be observed at every point. The structure as well as many details enable one to see Bultmann's
background in the history of religions school. He builds upon
the research of men such as Wrede, Heitmüller, and Bousset--
and frequently retains even their disputed conclusions. But
Bultmann has also assimilated the research of the last generation. The book's word studies, models of conciseness and precision, illustrate that Bultmann's Theology was written during
the period of publication of Kittel's Theological Dictionary.[3]
In contrast, the form-critical method has not affected the
work to the degree one might have expected.[4] He has little
regard for "typology," eagerly pursued by many scholars today.
He remains critical and judicious.

Yet for Bultmann critical and historical research is only
preliminary. The reconstruction of early Christian history
stands "in the service of the interpretation of the New Testament writings under the presupposition that they have something
to say to the present" (II, 251). By setting this course Bultmann distinguishes himself not only from the history of religions school but also from a scholar like Goguel. Goguel was a
historian who investigated the phenomena of early Christianity
in order to understand how religious experience led to the creation of a new religious object and functioned historically
through the development of theology and of social structures.

Bultmann's work (unlike, for example, Weinel's[5]) is properly titled Theology of the New Testament. His biblical theological approach is the element he shares with the whole theological renewal since World War I, associated with names such
as Barth and Gogarten.[6] However, this new orientation has not

meant for Bultmann a break with comparative religion; he, unlike many others, has succeeded in integrating theology and historical research. His work with the texts requires that faith be viewed in relation to its object, namely as faith in the kerygma. Faith cannot be conceived as a non-theoretical attitude (e.g., as cultic piety or as mysticism). As faith in the kerygma it always implies a specific understanding that becomes theologically explicit in historical situations.

The nature of New Testament theology demands that it be presented not as a dogmatic system, but in its historical development. It follows directly from the theology of the New Testament itself that no universally valid Christian dogmatic is possible. Each generation must face the theological task anew in the specificity of its historical situation. To replace a traditional dogmatic system with a system of Heilsgeschichte is not particularly helpful: Stauffer is reproached because he turns theology into a religious philosophy of history (II, 248). The center of the New Testament for Bultmann is not the "Christian understanding of time and history,"[7] but the message of the pardoning of sinners through God's act in Jesus Christ. Accordingly, the theological statements of the New Testament are the explication of the understanding founded in faith and given in specific historical situations. In this insight Bultmann follows A. Schlatter: the act of thinking and the act of living should not be separated (II, 237).

But even the addition of this reference to Schlatter does not complete the description of Bultmann's place in the history of biblical scholarship. Schlatter's concern was careful description, and he was guided by the belief that unbiased observation would disclose not only the life of the historical Jesus, but also the significance of the "History of Christ." Bultmann, in contrast, pursues the kerygma that is grasped only in faith

and the theological understanding that follows from it. Therefore, he must move from mere observation to putting questions
to the texts: How do they understand the kerygma? What understanding of God, man and the world does the kerygma provide?
This constant questioning of the texts is not merely a hermeneutical means to the establishment of what the scriptures
themselves say. The texts are also questioned as to how far
the theology implicitly and explicitly present in them is a
proper expression of the self-understanding of faith. Out of
the distinction and inter-relation of kerygma and theology
arises the task of content-criticism (II, 238f.). This understanding of the task springs neither from history of religions
research nor from the influence of Barth or Schlatter.

For his content-criticism Bultmann appeals to Luther and
to his criticism of the Epistle of James and of Revelation (II,
239). Bultmann's theology of the New Testament stands in a
tradition of the Reformation, specifically the Lutheran understanding of scripture.[8] Bultmann finds that content-criticism
is not only an abstract possibility but a real necessity. He
is led to this conclusion by his observation that traces of
the "Development Toward the Ancient Church" (par. 51-61) are
already present within the New Testament. I take his point to
be that the Catholicism of the early church cannot be criticized on the basis of the New Testament without criticizing
parts of the content of the New Testament itself. This cannot, in fact, be easily contradicted. Catholicism can hardly
be opposed with imitative biblicism. It appears today, therefore, that not only a liberal Catholicism of Anglican character, as is represented by F. C. Grant, but even Roman Catholicism is often more open to the historical investigation of the
New Testament than is a biblicizing Protestantism.

For Bultmann as for Luther the kerygma, or gospel, is the

point of orientation and the center of all theology. His
preference for Paul and John is genuinely Lutheran. Bultmann
obtains the criteria for his content-criticism from them. In
no recent biblical theology is the Pauline doctrine of justification made so pivotal and presented so impressively. It is
no accident that Bultmann's New Testament theology ends with
the ecclesiastical institution of penance, where Luther's reformation began. With his content-criticism he sets _Christum_
contra scripturam.[9]

It is natural to ask whether content-criticism should not
be a task of systematic theology rather than of New Testament
scholarship. Does not Bultmann cross the boundary between
biblical theology and systematic theology? In fact there is
no sharp line for him. Biblical theology leads him to the
limit where criticism stops and preaching begins, while
Goguel's presentation presses on to the threshold of philosophy of religion. However, the boundary is not crossed, at
least not intentionally. His interpretation sets forth the
understanding of human existence implied in the theological
statements of the New Testament. This is to him a scholarly
task. The interpretation of New Testament theological statements in the categories of existentialism should not be confused with existential knowledge of God.[10] But it is evident
that one cannot understand Bultmann's theology of the New Testament without considering his hermeneutical principles. These
in turn have their presupposition in a specific philosophical
analysis of human existence.

Therefore, Bultmann's presentation belongs to the category of philosophically determined interpretations of the New
Testament. It employs quite consciously a terminology stemming from a specific philosophical tradition. That must be
considered precisely by one who, like the reviewer, feels him-

self to be an outsider in relation to German philosophy. Although in his work on the problem of hermeneutics[11] he begins with Dilthey and Count Yorck von Wartenburg, he leaves no doubt that fundamentally he builds on the existential philosophy of Heidegger. Insight into the "historicity of existence" has decisively clarified the problem of understanding historical documents for him and appears to him to be the appropriate "pre-understanding" for the interpretation of the New Testament.

The philosophical presuppositions explain the terminology--often quite difficult for the non-German to understand--with which Bultmann interprets the New Testament. They also explain the somewhat "schoolmasterish" tone in which he questions the New Testament writings on their understanding of existence and criticizes their mythological views. He knows how to state not only what the New Testament writings say, but also what they express "in reality" (e.g., I, 259). He knows the real intention of Paul (I, 301) and can even further develop his thought (I, 253). His intention in this is neither to make dogmatic judgments nor to employ a particular theological method. Existential interpretation means, rather, that the writings of the New Testament are to be questioned as to how they understand human existence in history. In the same way, all classical historical phenomena are to be questioned and interpreted in terms of their understanding of existence. Bultmann himself has impressively done this in his _Primitive Christianity_ in relation to the Old Testament and Judaism, Hellenic culture and Hellenism.[12]

Bultmann brings three questions to the New Testament: (1) Does it present a unique understanding of existence? (2) What is the specificity of this understanding? (3) Is this understanding of existence a possibility for contemporary

95

man? He finds that a new self-understanding in faith is made
possible through the kerygma and is developed by Paul and
John. Therefore content-criticism is a legitimate scientific
enterprise. It deals with the question whether this specifically Christian self-understanding is retained or abandoned in
the other New Testament writings.

Bultmann asks what the writings of the New Testament have
to say to the present through what they said in their specific
historical situations. Thus, not only the kerygma but also
the believing self-understanding made possible by it is to
some extent extricated from the concrete historical limitation
present in the New Testament. For as Bultmann views the theology of the New Testament, the facts of the history both of
Jesus and of early Christianity, like "mythological" cosmol-
ogy, eschatology, and Christology, are meaningful only insofar
as they can illuminate the understanding of existence. The
connection of the "act of thinking" with the "act of living,"
taken concretely by Schlatter, is traced to a prior understanding of the historicity of existence. The theology of the New
Testament is presented not as historically given but as existentially significant. One can therefore say: the New Testament is dehistoricized; and one will have to ask whether this
dehistoricizing of the New Testament is not more characteristic for the theology of Bultmann than the famous demythologizing, which is certainly but another side of the same concern.

In this respect Bultmann approximates the Enlightenment,
which in the interpretation of the New Testament laid aside
"everything local and temporal, everything individual and particular" (II, 243). Certainly he does not seek to extract
timeless, universal truths; he seeks to determine the new possibility of understanding human existence by distilling it out
of concrete history. Thus he stands nearer to F. C. Baur, for

96

whom the philosophy of Hegel rendered a service similar to that which Heidegger renders for Bultmann. A parallel phenomenon, again from different philosophical presuppositions, is the Swedish Lundensian theology represented by A. Nygren in his *Agape* and *Eros*, in which the writings of the New Testament and the history of doctrine were examined for the basic motif lying behind the concrete statements.

In some way we all depend upon philosophical traditions. Certainly, important advances in New Testament historical research often have been associated with philosophical reflection. One cannot deny that existential philosophy--itself influenced by Christian tradition--can render worthwhile services in the interpretation of the New Testament. Bultmann is not forced by his philosophical presuppositions to lose sight of the kerygma and thereby to eliminate it, as did Baur and the theology of the Enlightenment. In relation to Nygren, Bultmann has an advantage, since it is easier for him to clarify how the gospel frees man from the law. Moreover, the connection with Heidegger has helped him to break through and to correct the earlier dominant understanding of New Testament anthropology that was determined by idealistic tradition. Yet, by embracing existential philosophy he sets forth the theological statements of the New Testament only in a peculiarly anthropological metamorphosis. The question arises whether or not Bultmann absolutizes his philosophical "pre-understanding" in such a way that he decides in advance what the New Testament writings may or may not really say.

The lineage of Bultmann's theology can be traced in quite diverse directions. One cannot, however, speak of eclecticism. Bultmann's theology is a syncretistic phenomenon only in the same sense as is the Johannine, in which also--at least if we should believe Bultmann--very distinct traditions are worked

into a consistent unity. The inner consistency of this presentation is impressive; it is almost uncanny. It seems to
rest on a kind of preestablished harmony of critical biblical
study, Reformation faith, and modern existential philosophy.
A defect at one point might easily make the whole impressive
structure totter.

It is not easy to enter into genuine dialog with the
work. That a circular method is present is easily verified.
The hermeneutical propriety of the existential approach is
demonstrated by New Testament theology which is in turn existentially interpreted. However, that need not be a vicious
circle; it could also be a legitimate hermeneutical circle.
For the decisive test of any hermeneutical method lies in its
appropriateness in relation to the text to be interpreted.
This test presupposes an exegesis of the text, while the exegesis already assumes a hermeneutical method. However, Bultmann works out the interrelation with such consistency that
the result appears to be a closed system, bewildering at least
one observer.

What has been said about the place of the work within the
history of research enables us to make a preliminary evaluation
of the book's worth. The principal achievement of Bultmann's
Theology of the New Testament is that it both differentiates
and co-relates kerygma and theology; the theological statements
are understood as an explication of faith in the face of specific historical challenges. Thus, the separation of the "act
of thinking" from the "act of living" is avoided. Thereby two
misunderstandings of the New Testament are overcome: orthodox
and rationalistic intellectualism, and the anti-intellectual-
ism of the liberals and of the history of religions school.
In this regard, one can only hope that subsequent work will
not fall short of this achievement.

The main problems of Bultmann's work arise from the exis-
tentialistic interpretation of the theology of the New Testament in terms of man's new self-understanding and the conse-
quent dehistoricization of the New Testament. Discussion with
Bultmann has to focus on this point.[13] This review can only
make a beginning by substantiating and elucidating these two
theses.

The Outline of the Book

The outline of the work is clear. In the center stands
the theology of Paul (I, 185-352); it serves as the point of
historical orientation, and greatest stress falls on it. The
centrality of Paul may be seen by what Bultmann relegates to
"Presuppositions and Motifs of New Testament Theology": "The
Message of Jesus" (I, 3-32), "The Kerygma of the Earliest Church"
(I, 33-62), and "The Kerygma of the Hellenistic Church aside from
Paul" (I, 63-183). "The Theology of the Gospel of John and the
Johannine Epistles" stands independently beside Paul (II, 3-92).
A fourth and final section deals with "The Development toward
the Ancient Church": "The Rise of Church Order and Its Earliest
Development," (II, 95-118), "The Development of Doctrine" (II,
119-154), "Christology and Soteriology (II, 155-202), and "The
Problem of Christian Living" (II, 203-236).

A glance at the table of contents shows that in one respect Bultmann's work carries out the program advanced by
Wrede.[14] Moreover, one is reminded of Bousset's _Kyrios Chris-_
tos. What Bousset had presented in monograph form, Bultmann
carries through for the whole of New Testament theology. By
choosing one option, Bultmann has succeeded in presenting both
the unity and the diversity of the New Testament. He thus
masters this persistent problem of New Testament theology.
The unity lies in the determinative importance of the kerygma

for theology throughout the New Testament. Furthermore, all New Testament writings presuppose not only Jesus and the earliest church, but also the development of Christianity in Hellenistic communities. The post-Pauline writings all belong in some way to the development toward the ancient church and are in various ways affected by the same questions. Above all, between John and Paul, Bultmann finds an intimate, essential affinity (II, 6f.).

The outline of the work itself reveals a preference for Pauline and Johannine theology. In a certain sense only in the Pauline and Johannine writings can one speak of a comprehensive and consistent theological perspective. This was already observed by Wrede, but Bultmann has gone further: the close relation of believing self-understanding to the kerygma is explicit only in Pauline and Johannine theology. Bultmann's arrangement tends toward undue neglect of the theology of the other New Testament writings. It is striking that the theological perspectives implicit in Matthew, Mark, and Luke-Acts, are only indicated but not really analysed.

Bultmann begins his book with the proposition that: "The message of Jesus is a presupposition for the theology of the New Testament rather than a part of that theology itself." There are no good reasons to object at this point. The history of religions school had already recognized that New Testament Christianity could neither be identified with the religion of Jesus nor be derived directly from it.[15] The kerygma of Jesus Christ, the crucified and risen one, is the foundation of the whole theology of the New Testament, including that of the Gospels. The preaching of Jesus isolated from this kerygma and critically reconstructed is only a presupposition. Yet the words and work of Jesus do belong to the theology of the New Testament insofar as (and in the forms in which) they were

handed on by the church, interpreted, and presented in the
Gospels. To be sure, the substance and the consequences of
the Christian faith could be developed with little attention
to any details of Jesus' life, as was done by Paul. But what
characterizes the New Testament is the inclusion of Gospels
as well as epistles. Certainly the Gospels too may be ap-
proached with questions concerning the understanding of existence that they imply. But this understanding is expressed
only in an indirect way. The direct unfolding of the kerygma
takes the form of stories about what Jesus said and did as
recollected and interpreted by Christian faith. This interpretation of Jesus' history should be closely analyzed in a
theology of the New Testament.[16] Bultmann does not feel
obliged to do so because he sees the theology of the New Testament to be statements concerning believing existence; but in
view of the sources, this is quite one-sided. Bultmann ab-
stracts the eschatological kerygma from the history of Jesus
presented and interpreted in the Gospels and dehistoricizes it
in ultra-Pauline fashion. This is clear even in the outline
of the work.

Bultmann does recognize that the message of Jesus, precisely because it is his message, is not only historically
antecedent to but also a necessary presupposition for New Testament theology. For this reason he deals with it in his work.
In an analogous way, perhaps, the Old Testament, as the Holy
Scripture presupposed by the New Testament writers, ought to
have been discussed. That is not necessary for Bultmann because he finds no necessary connection between the kerygma and
the Old Testament, nor does he see the kerygma within a comprehensive perspective of salvation history (for which he
appeals to John, cf. e.g., II, 122). In general, though significant non-biblical parallel material is presupposed, it is

101

cited only occasionally. In this respect the book <u>Primitive</u> <u>Christianity</u> <u>in</u> <u>its</u> <u>Contemporary</u> <u>Setting</u> is a valuable supplement to the larger work. But here as well Bultmann deals less with historical details than with the essential characteristics of Judaism, Greek culture, and early Christianity. These are somewhat systematized but sharply, suggestively, and clearly worked out.

Thus the main questions that are to be raised with respect to the organization of Bultmann's book are at the same time questions about his interpretation of the New Testament. It may be said parenthetically that Bultmann's ordering of the material, like any other order, leaves some difficulties unresolved. It turns out to be impossible to distinguish clearly between the "Hellenistic Church Aside from Paul" and "The Development Toward the Ancient Church." For example, the material treated in par. 11, "The Church's Relation to Judaism and the Problem of the Old Testament," properly belongs to the post-Pauline period.

The History of Primitive Christianity

Bultmann brings a precise description of the history of primitive Christianity into the service of existential interpretation. The picture drawn by Bultmann is naturally dependent on earlier critical research and offers no great surprises. But here, as in his earlier works, Bultmann has also made original contributions to historical reconstruction. It is not simply a synthesis of prior achievements. In questions of introduction he is critical; the difference from H. J. Holtzmann is not very great. However, unlike Goguel, for example, he has freed himself from Baur's image of early Christian history and builds on the work of the German history of religions school. The stress on pre-Pauline hellenistic Christianity is remarkable; so is the judgment that the Johannine writings are not dependent on Paul (II, 3ff.). It is also important for the historical picture that Bultmann emphasizes, with more recent research, the significance of eschatology for the whole of primitive Christianity. This eschatological context is important for his understanding both of the kerygma and of the church. At such points one notes how much has happened in New Testament research from Bousset to Bultmann. Even if Bultmann emphasizes the changes in the understanding of existence from Jesus to the ancient church, the historical continuity that connects them is more easily seen in his work than in Bousset's. The decisive problems were largely present, though latent, in the church from the beginning (e.g., I, 118 and 121).

The message of Jesus is delineated in essentially the same way as in Jesus and the Word.[17] His presentation is impressive, even to one who might disagree on many points.[18] In the Theology, Jesus' messianic self-consciousness is handled in some detail. With Wrede, it is still answered negatively. The methodological problems of any quest for the historical Jesus become particularly evident at this point. Detailed criticism and overall judgment of tradition are joined together. The extremely complicated questions cannot, however, be discussed here.

However, for a comprehensive evaluation of Bultmann's biblical theology, it is important to see that the negative result on this point really means a positive gain for his existential interpretation. The conclusion that Jesus did not claim to be the Messiah precludes the possibility that Jesus' messiahship is a historically establishable fact. Only in the decision of faith is Jesus to be apprehended as the revealer and Savior. For Bultmann, historical criticism, which makes it impossible to draw a picture of Jesus' personality, serves

103

to deny faith any historical security. As the preacher and as
the one preached, Jesus' person signifies the demand for decision. According to Bultmann, no confirmable data mitigate the
skandalon of the Word. This explains why Jesus' messianic
self-consciousness, as well as his whole history, is regarded
as theologically irrelevant. To the evangelists, however,
Jesus' history is not an indifferent matter, though they also
know the offense: the hidden glory of this history is only
visible to faith. My question to Bultmann is: Does he not
avoid the offense given with the concrete history of Jesus and
thereby also lose sight of the glory, visible to faith, in
this history? The kerygma isolated from Jesus' history is in
danger of becoming a paradox without content.

His description of the earliest church is also dependent
on the method employed. Anyone who describes the Jerusalem
church proceeds by inferences. But there is a wide gulf between what must go back to the primitive community and what
may possibly go back to it. As with the quest for the historical Jesus, it would be appropriate to clarify the maximal
as well as the minimal limits in order to approach the historical facts from both sides.[19] Like Bousset, Bultmann tends to
utilize only that material which can be critically established
with near certitude. Bultmann makes no use of the history of
later Jewish Christianity, which provides relevant but difficult opportunities for comparison.[20]

It is worth noting that Bultmann stresses that the earliest church understood itself as the eschatological community
and that tendencies toward the development of ecclesiastical
forms, traditions, succession, etc. already existed. The view
that the dominant title of Jesus was Son of Man (I, 49) seems
questionable to me; it is found almost solely in sayings attributed to Jesus. The use of the name "Christ" in the Pauline

epistles presupposes that the title "Messiah" stood at the center of the oldest kerygma.[21] This is confirmed by the passion narratives, for they also focus on Jesus as King of the Jews. The scriptural proof for the messiahship and suffering of Jesus must have been developed in the earliest church. The traditional testimonies in the New Testament, therefore, should have been used more extensively in the description of its kerygma.[22]

With Bousset, Bultmann denies that Jesus could have been culticly venerated by the earliest Palestinian church (I, 50). Nevertheless, he leaves more room for the possibility that Jesus was thought already to exercise his kingly authority from heaven. He refers, among other texts, to Matthew 11:22f; 16:17-19; 18-20. Further, he assumes, at this point with less skepticism than Goguel, that the earliest church knew that the Spirit had been given to it (I, 41). He does not deny that the name of Jesus was invoked, at least in exorcism. It is only a small step to assert that exclamations of homage and supplication as well were directed to the exalted Messiah, Jesus. The contention that the _Maranatha_ exclamations could originally have been addressed to God (I, 51f.) seems to me a mere expedient. It is true that the absolute _kyrios_ has no direct counterpart in Semitic usage. Yet the very framing of the question--whether the _kyrios_ cult existed on Palestinian soil or not--is hardly suited to clarify the attitude of the earliest church to its exalted Messiah.[23]

The contributions made in the section "The Kerygma of the Hellenistic Church aside from Paul" go far beyond Bousset. Such a comprehensive picture of Christianity before and alongside Paul has not been previously drawn. Bultmann isolates traditional material primarily by lexical and form critical analysis of the Pauline and non-Pauline writings. The endeav-

or is extremely suggestive and fruitful. Much remains hypothetical but it could hardly be otherwise. It might be interesting to compare Bultmann's attempt with those of British and
American scholars, independent of Bultmann and largely unknown
to him.

The use of the term "kerygma" in the heading fits only
part of the content of the section and can promote a common
misuse of the word. What makes Hellenistic Christianity relevant for Bultmann is the kerygma at its core. To this extent,
his use of the word "kerygma" in the chapter heading is justified. Yet the result is a certain one-sidedness. Preaching
to the community is not to be characterized as kerygma; it
should have been possible to give a fuller picture through
analyses of forms, patterns, and ideas. Further, more could
have been said concerning the use of christological formulas
in confession, prayer, and thanksgiving. That the kerygma
evokes not only believing understanding but also confession
and thanksgiving, praise of God and Christ, is insufficiently
treated in the book as a whole (yet cf. II, 155).

In his treatment of the sacraments, Bultmann seems too
dependent on Heitmüller's important but dated work. The
naming of Jesus' name as an independent sacrament concurrent
with baptism (I, 137) can be derived neither from Paul nor
from Luke nor from liturgical history. That baptism was per-
formed in the name of Jesus expresses rather the relation of
water baptism to the kerygma. This relation is not established by the interpretation given Romans 6 but is its presupposition.

Seen from outside, early Hellenistic Christianity is a
"syncretistic phenomenon" for Bultmann.[24] He emphasizes
Gnostic influence even more strongly than Bousset. Bultmann
correctly makes a sharper distinction than Reitzenstein

between mystery religions and Gnosticism. Because he sees a new understanding of existence emerging in pre-Christian and in Christian Gnosticism,[25] Bultmann assigns Gnosticism much greater historical significance than do historians of religion such as M. P. Nilsson or A. D. Nock who work more empirically, using archeological evidence. It remains, however, an open question whether or not one may speak of a homogeneous Gnostic movement, of a religion taking form in individual groups and congregations (I, 167). Bultmann's reference to the Qumran manuscripts as sources of a pre-Christian Gnosticizing Judaism (II, 13) only makes this question more urgent.[26] The whole complex of problems will have to be worked through anew on the basis of the Qumran and Nag Hammadi documents.[27]

The Development toward the Ancient Church

As an outline of historical development, the fourth section, "The Development toward the Ancient Church," is closely connected with the first. Here too, Bultmann makes important contributions. He stresses that ministry constitutes the ancient church; ecclesiastical order acquires divine sanction. Bultmann picks up the discussion between Harnack and Sohm on which he makes the perceptive comment: "Harnack focuses upon the Ecclesia as historical phenomenon; Sohm understands it from the point of view of its own understanding of itself" (II, 96). Bultmann brings to light the underlying problems and this can contribute substantially to their clarification. For example, his distinction between a regulative and a constitutive significance of church law is valuable.

It is questionable whether or not the apostles are properly to be termed charismatic leaders (II, 103f.). As Bultmann himself stresses, the apostle is the one who has been commissioned. Apostles are to be designated as charismatics

107

only in the specifically Pauline sense whereby even everyday
community activities are considered charismatic (1 Cor. 12:28).
The distinction between the original meaning of apostle, messenger of Christ in the end time, and its later assessment,
initiator of a stream of tradition, could possibly have been
sharpened.

The paragraphs on "Paradosis and Historical Tradition"
and "The Problem of Right Teaching" (Par. 54 and 55) are extremely suggestive. The incisive formulations compel thorough
reflection. In a certain sense, the whole of Bultmann's work
revolves around the problem of revelation and history. The
problem stems from the special character of paradosis, that it
speaks of an event, at once eschatological and historical (II,
121ff.). Both Matthew and Mark express the paradox, though in
different ways. But in Luke-Acts, Bultmann finds that the
paradox has been resolved in the interest of a theology of
history. This criticism of the Lukan writings makes clear the
way in which Bultmann "dehistoricizes" the New Testament.

Luke, unlike Paul, is interested in a "Life of Jesus";
eschatological awareness fades away and is replaced by a consciousness of standing within a continuing history of salvation. However, Bultmann goes too far when he claims that Luke
understands Christianity as "a new religion" and as "an entity
of world history" (II, 116f.). The chronological notices imply
little more than that Jesus lived at a definite point of time
in world history. Acts is not simply an account of the establishment and early history of the Christian community. Its
intention is rather to report the growth of the Word. The active Word, not a chronological inter-connection of cause and
effect, provides the continuity of history. Therefore, the
speeches do not have the same significance as those of the
ancient historians. Moreover, Acts is not so isolated in the

New Testament as Bultmann thinks. The Pauline epistles attest
that the church which understood itself as an eschatological
community was not uninterested in reports concerning the Jerusalem church or in the expansion of Christianity, and so forth
(cf., e.g., 1 Thess. 2:14; 1:6ff.; Rom. 1:8; Gal. 1:23). Stories about Jesus have such an organic place in preaching that
one should not regard historical tradition and preaching as
antithetical.

Certainly, the first volume of Luke-Acts is not strictly
speaking a Gospel. It is a narrative about the event whose
saving significance the apostolic kerygma proclaims. The second volume is an account of the apostolic preaching which
brought this kerygma to the Gentiles. The note of eschatological fulfillment is clearly sounded in both parts of the work
(Luke 4:16ff. and Acts 2:16ff. are programmatic for each volume). Luke, like Matthew and Mark, knows that men's eyes are
opened to the saving significance of Jesus' history by the
appearances of the Risen Christ (Luke 24:44ff.). However, the
mere existence of Luke's two volume work indicates that he
does not perceive as paradox the historicity of the saving
event. This is the heart of Bultmann's objection to Luke.
But did primitive Christianity identify the eschatological
events with the end of history as Bultmann assumes? The
eschaton implies the end of the present course of time, but at
least for a more naive view, that does not mean the end of all
temporality and of history.[28] From this perspective a historical event may well have eschatological significance. The
problem was located elsewhere; without the revelation of the
Risen Christ and the testimony of the Spirit, it was impossible
to see eschatological significance in Jesus' history. If I
understand correctly, Bultmann judges Luke-Acts by the standards of a profane scientific historiography and a dehistori-

cized eschatology, both of which are foreign to the author, instead of understanding Luke's work from his own much more "naive" outlook. Bultmann has censored Luke, not given him a chance to speak. But we must grant that this is a logical consequence of his total approach.[29]

The discussion of the various theological perspectives found within late canonical and early post-canonical writings focuses on "Christology and Soteriology" (Par. 58). The inclusion of the apostolic fathers enables us to see more clearly the tendencies of developing tradition. He approaches the texts with the question: how is the relation of present to future salvation understood? Closely connected is the question of the relation of indicative to imperative, which stands in the foreground in the section on "The Problem of Christian Living" (Par. 59-61). It is characteristic of the developing church that the general tendency is toward the disappearance of the understanding that existence is totally renewed in faith. In the same way, the meaning of the eschatological "interim" is lost. The radical fallenness of man enslaved by sin is no longer seen and the meaning of baptism is limited to forgiveness of past sins. Legalism creeps in and cannot be overcome by the sacramental emphasis. The imperative is understood moralistically; this is noticeable in a number of concrete demands. As the discipline of penance is institutionalized, the church becomes an institution of salvation.

Great differences exist among the individual writings. What is striking is Bultmann's positive evaluation of Ignatius. In his way he expressed the totaliter-aliter of the new existence and understood faith to involve the whole being and the whole doing of the believer (existentiell). Bultmann stresses that there is a strong Pauline influence within Colossians, Ephesians, and the Pastorals; even Barnabas comes off rather well. In general, however, the writings are quite sharply criticized on the basis of existentially interpreted Pauline and Johannine theology.

But to what degree is it legitimate to judge these writings by standards extracted from Paul and John? Bultmann writes: "Both in terminology and in substance it is the influence of the synagogue that is here at work pushing aside the theology of Paul (and of John)" (II, 215). But may one speak of a "pushing aside?" Writings such as Hebrews and Barnabas, James and the Didache, 1 Clement and Hermas are affected only in a very superficial way, if at all, by specifically Pauline or Johannine theology. These writings draw on traditions which stem from early Christian circles distinct from those of Paul and John. Bultmann seems not to have freed himself radically enough from the old tradition of purely documentary research. The writings are so quickly examined and judged in terms of Paul and John that insufficient attention is paid to what they themselves have to say.

This is especially clear in the case of Hebrews. The fundamental conception here is entirely different from Paul. Paul awaits a new creation through the eschatological act of God and sees it already realized in Christ. In contrast, for the author of Hebrews the world to come was created "from the foundation of the world" (4:3); it exists already in heaven. Accordingly, eschatological salvation does not mean that man becomes a new creation, but only that he enters the heavenly-eschatological world. The event is described in cultic categories; salvation is not being pronounced righteous, but being granted free access to God in worship. With this wholly different orientation it makes little sense to state that the Pauline antitheses _pistis_ - _erga_ and _charis_ - _erga_ are absent, or that there is no mention of dying and rising with Christ,

111

or that there are only traditional statements about the Spirit (II, 168).

This premature comparison with Paul has the consequence that even Hebrews' "understanding of existence" is prejudiced. Bultmann sees that the believer is proleptically placed into heavenly existence through baptism and is thereby freed from the world (II, 167-8). But he relates Hebrews' rejection of a second repentance much too closely to its affirmation by Hermas. In Hebrews, the impossibility of a new conversion is a necessary consequence of the singular finality of the forgiveness of sins in the death of Christ and is asserted paraenetically, not as a canon of church discipline. The life of the believer stands primarily under the promise rather than under the demand of God. For Christians who already share in eschatological existence and who live on earth only as strangers, the present is an interim in more than the chronological sense. Because Christ has made entrance into the sanctuary possible for them, "they should draw near with a true heart" (10:19ff.). This summons touches their whole manner of life. Thus the imperative is really grounded in the indicative, even though the relation is not dialectical or paradoxical in the same way as it is in Paul.

Details may be debated. The fundamental question, illustrated by our discussion of Hebrews, is this: Does Bultmann prematurely apply a standard extracted from Paul and John to other early Christian writings? But to assess the whole work, we must judge whether or not Bultmann has correctly interpreted Pauline and Johannine theology.

The Interpretation of Pauline Theology

The division "The Theology of Paul" moves beyond mere description to profound interpretation. It is a great achieve-

ment. It represents the center of the work in more than an
external way. The correlation of kerygma and believing understanding and the resulting conception of what constitutes New
Testament theology are derived primarily from Paul. That is
why Paul provides Bultmann with his principal standard for
evaluating other New Testament writings.

Yet it is necessary to make it clear from the beginning
that even Paul's theology is not simply empirically described.
Bultmann's principal concern is to interpret the basic theological position which is the foundation for Paul's specific
statements (I, 190). The essence of Paul's theology is more
or less distilled from these concrete expressions within their
historical setting. The abstraction of this theological position is achieved in two ways: 1. Bultmann largely ignores
the specific historical challenges in response to which Paul
developed his theology, even the basic fact that Paul became
the founder of a Christian theology precisely as an apostle to
the Gentiles; 2. Bultmann looks for what is characteristic of
Pauline theology, further divesting it of historical concrete-
ness. He thinks he must criticize Paul's statements by Paul's
intention.

Bultmann presents Pauline theology as anthropology, ar-
ranging the material under two headings: 1. Man prior to the
revelation of faith; 2. Man under faith. Existentialist leanings are obvious. Yet the arrangement is appropriate to the
material. It corresponds to the outline of Romans as well as
to the preaching pattern ("once you were... but now you are...")
identified by Bultmann (I, 105f.). Naturally these patterns
have as their presupposition the kerygma, which Bultmann set
forth in the section on the Hellenistic community. It is an
obvious advantage for Bultmann that this section has already
dealt with traditional materials in Paul's letters. Thus

113

Bultmann has freed himself from treating such traditions as an integral part of Paul's theology; he can vigorously and impressively pursue the main line of specifically Pauline thought. But this method of Bultmann's is questionable in that it enables him to reduce the meaning of common Christian tradition for the theology of Paul to the mere that of the kerygma. In this way, Bultmann's arrangement involves from the outset a critical stance toward the theology present in the epistles. It is true that Paul does not begin Romans with an extended statement of the "salvation occurrence" (I, 301). The reason is simply that he presupposes the Roman congregation to be informed. Thus the brief reference in 1:2-4 is an adequate reminder.

The section "Man prior to the Revelation of Faith" begins with a treatment of Paul's anthropological concepts. This treatment yields a formal analysis of the ontological structure of human existence (I, 191-227). At this point Bultmann's existentialist leanings are especially clear. There are some good reasons for this arrangement. Paul's theological statements do indeed have presuppositions which are not expressed because they were self-evident to him. Analysis of his anthropological concepts contributes to the clarification of such presuppositions. What is objectionable is the limitation to anthropological ideas, so that something like an existentialist analysis of the structures of existence emerges. Bultmann himself knows not only that "Paul's theology is at the same time anthropology" (I, 191), but also that any statement about man speaks "about man as he is qualified by the divine deed and demand and by his attitude toward them" (I, 191). The divine existence of God is a presupposition just as self-evident for Paul as the human existence of man. The God who addresses man in the kerygma is not an unknown God for Paul,

114

but the Creator, already known from the Old Testament, who
directs history and who is himself its goal. Bultmann mentions
this (I, 228f.), but with extraordinary brevity.

It is impossible in a review to do justice to the richness
of Bultmann's presentation. Following the paragraphs on
"Flesh, Sin and the World," a section on the dikaiosynē theou
opens the chapter of "Man under Faith." It is noteworthy--and
not just because of the contrast to Bousset and Wrede--that
the doctrine of justification is strongly emphasized. In a
purely descriptive presentation such a concentration would be
one-sided. However, Bultmann's presentation is not affected
by such an objection, for Paul's essential concern is expressed
nowhere so clearly as in the doctrine of justification. It is
basic to Bultmann's understanding that dikaiosynē is here a
forensic-eschatological term. It is not a quality of man, but
signifies his relation to God. This is worked out very clearly.

Bultmann's criticism of Mundle[30] clarifies the fundamental
significance of the doctrine of justification: the works of
the law represent human achievements in general. Paul sets
forth his doctrine of justification in his debate with Jews
and Judaizers. Yet the polemic against works righteousness
has a parallel in the polemic against the Greeks; they seek a
wisdom of their own in order to have something about which to
boast. In this Bultmann is quite right. Mundle's interpretation is correct only insofar as a Christian legalism not
appealing to the Mosaic law was not an actual, conscious problem for the apostle. If this is the case with Paul, it is
understandable that legalism was not seen as a problem in the
post-Pauline period. Again Bultmann detaches the fundamental
meaning of Paul's theology from its historical situation.
This is also clear in his whole treatment of the law (I, 259-69).

In Paul the law confronts men as the Mosaic law. Accord-

ing to Bultmann's interpretation, this is significant only
insofar as it shows that the law is understood by Paul not as
an ideal moral law but as a command of God demanding obedience
in the concrete situation. What Paul had to say concerning
the place of the law in pre-Christian epochs silently falls
victim to critical interpretation. It is even more remarkable
that Bultmann, for whom the argument of Romans 1-8 is so basic,
has almost nothing to say concerning Romans 9-11. But does
not a descriptive exegetical approach suggest that chapters 9-
11 are central to Paul's principle concern in writing to the
Roman Christians? However, according to Bultmann, the mystery
of the history of salvation in these chapters is derived from
"speculative fantasy" (II, 132) and is theologically irrelevant. Bultmann convincingly locates the center of Paul's theology in the doctrine of the justification of sinners through
the grace of God, and he explicates all Paul's thought from
this perspective. But Bultmann slights the historical data
when he isolates the doctrine of justification from the framework of salvation history and from futuristic eschatology.

The question of the relation between the history of salvation and believing self-understanding becomes acute in
"Christ's Death and Resurrection as Salvation-occurrence"
(par. 33). This section illustrates Bultmann's claim that the
task of demythologizing is raised by the New Testament itself.[31]
The problem arises because Paul understands the grace of God
not as an attribute of God but rather as an act of God. It is
the event in which God bestows on man the gift of grace, radically transforming the human situation. But at the same time
this act of grace, this salvation-occurrence, embraces the
death and resurrection of Jesus.

Bultmann first of all traces the use of the various terms
by which Paul expresses the saving significance of the cross.

He finds them problematical because they can all lead to the view that believing submission to the grace of God is dependent on a previous acceptance of the reported data of salvation. According to the true intention of Paul, however, "the decision-question whether a man is willing to give up his old understanding of himself and henceforth understand himself only from the grace of God and the question whether he will acknowledge Jesus Christ as the Son of God and Lord should turn out to be one and the same question" (I, 300-301). To see that for Paul the Crucified One was the pre-existent Son of God and that the resurrection of Jesus was taken to be an established fact, makes the problem even more pressing.

Bultmann finds the answer in Paul's idea that the salvation occurrence continues to take place in the preaching of the Word: "the salvation-occurrence is nowhere present except in the proclaiming, accosting, demanding, and promising word of preaching" (I, 302). The references to the incarnation of the pre-existent one are mythological expressions of the fact that "there exists a divinely authorized proclamation of the prevenient grace and love of God" (I, 305). Similarly, the resurrection--rather, the Resurrected One--is said to be "present in the proclaiming Word" (I, 305). It is quite clear to Bultmann himself that his exclusive concentration on this point is not a complete portrait of Paul, but a critical interpretation. The question is how far it actually does justice to the intention of the apostle.

Bultmann's concern is that the character of faith is genuine decision and the inner unity of the concept of faith must be preserved. The kerygma must be understood as address, and that is not possible, according to Bultmann, if it is understood as an account of demonstrable (or non-demonstrable) data, or as a communication of objective knowledge. Whether the

117

data that are held to be true by objectivizing thought are of a historical or mythological kind really makes no difference. "Demythologizing" and "dehistoricizing" are two aspects of the same protest against objectivizing language. Bultmann rejects such language as inadequate to the theological enterprise. Paul himself has given no account of the difference between objectivizing and existential thought; this is a task for the scholarly interpreter. Thus, his interpretation must be a critical one.

Bultmann's contention that man encounters the salvation-event in the kerygma and is summoned to decision, accurately reflects Paul's thought; so does the contention that the preaching of the salvation-event is itself part of the salva-tion-event (cf. 2 Cor. 5:18-6:2). Bultmann is also faithful to Paul when he maintains that knowledge of the salvation-event is distorted if it is thought to pertain to objective data and propositions to which one can subscribe without sur-rendering his unbelieving self-understanding. Historical and dogmatic insight, faith that works miracles, gifts of grace, charitable acts and heroic self-giving--these will all be cor-rupted if they become the occasion for unloving self-assertion (1 Cor. 1-4, 8, 13). The saving significance of Christ's death is only recognized when his death is understood to take place for us, that is "for my brother" as well as "for me." In this way, the death of Christ leads to a new self-under-standing. Accordingly, the kerygma is understood properly only when it is understood as address.

The decisive question at this point is whether or not the kerygma, if it is to be understood as personal address, can be at the same time a communication of information. Bultmann tends to see an exclusive antithesis. That, however, is not Pauline. Rather, the apostle thinks that the kerygma is a summons to faith precisely because it reports an event that happened prior to any human decision made in response to preaching. The prior event as the eschatological act of God is nevertheless absolutely decisive for the existence of man. Only because it is preached to him can man know the saving significance of this event, and only by sacrificing his former self-understanding can he believe truly; otherwise he would show that his faith is not genuine. But that does not mean that the event becomes salvation-occurrence only because it is preached.

God is not visible apart from faith, but it does not follow, as Bultmann himself has emphasized elsewhere, that apart from faith God does not exist.[32] In the same way, the saving act of God in Christ is visible only to faith; but this is not to say that only preaching and faith make the Christ-event the saving act of God. It is God's saving act apart from our faith and before our preaching. This is what Paul expresses when he depicts the death of Christ as expiatory sacrifice, substitution, cosmic event, etc. It is also expressed when, in opposition to the Gnostics at Corinth, he adduces evidence for the historicity of the resurrection.

The essential and unrelinquishable _extra_ _nos_ of righteousness and salvation in the theology of Paul seems to me to demand that the salvation-event be viewed as a once for all event of the past, not simply as a here and now occurrence present through preaching. If we are to speak of an event which has a dimension beyond human self-understanding, we can hardly avoid using categories of objectivizing thought. Since the Christ-event is proclaimed not as a this-worldly fact but as an eschatological act of God, how could Paul have spoken other than "mythologically"--even if the language of existentialism had been available?

119

Pauline theology is detached from faith as an existential attitude and falls prey to objectivizing thought when Paul's images of the cross' saving meaning are systematized into a scholastic theory of atonement, or when the evidence for the resurrection of Jesus is rationalized into a pseudo-scientific proof. Precisely in their more naive and fragmentary form Paul's "mythological" statements seem to me an appropriate reference to the _extra_ _nos_ of salvation. They express his true intention, and ought not to be interpreted away by the critic.

Naturally, the use of categories of objectivizing thought can always lead to misunderstanding. Rational assent can be confused with genuine faith. Theological wisdom can become a ground for boasting (kauchēma). Paul struggles against such deviations. But one cannot escape this danger by understanding the kerygma in an exclusive way as address and by interpreting the theological statements existentially. Existentialist understanding can be confused with true faith just as easily as dogmatic orthodoxy can.

To emphasize that the decisive salvation-occurrence has already happened in Christ apart from us and prior to preaching is not to make surrender to God's grace dependent on previous acceptance of the data of salvation. It is true that the surrender of faith occurs when a man is confronted by the gospel as a promising and demanding address; the salvation event is represented to him through baptism and is made concrete through the ministry of the preacher and the existence of the community. But the "objective" presupposition for this is that the salvation-event has already happened prior to preaching and independent of the community. Above all, the preacher must know that the grace of God in Christ is also bestowed apart from preaching. This must also be made clear in

the theological explication of believing understanding, even
if all knowledge remains imperfect.

Now Bultmann is aware of the _extra nos_, as his interpretation of the doctrine of justification shows. His rejection
of tendencies toward historicizing and mythologizing is a matter of his passionate religious concern: the kerygma must be
rescued from objectivizing thought which puts it at man's disposal, thus safeguarding the _extra nos_. Nevertheless, the
extra nos is endangered if the kerygma is reduced to the bare
that of the cross. This becomes clear in Bultmann's analysis
of the idea of faith (I, 314-30). Just as Bultmann characterized the kerygma as personal address, so here he characterizes
faith as decision. The emphasis on decision is so strong that
it is not made sufficiently clear that faith does not save because it is obedient and involves a new self-understanding,
but because it is faith in Jesus Christ.

Finally, I must raise the question whether or not Jesus
Christ remains a person in Bultmann's existential interpretation. Is there not a danger that the eschatological event
designated by the name Jesus Christ evaporates to a mere occurrence? In any case Bultmann's fear of a romantic category of
personality on the one hand and of mythological conceptualiza-
tion on the other leads to a lack of clarity at this point.
For Paul, the personhood of Jesus Christ is beyond any doubt.
Indeed, the Crucified One is identical with the Exalted and
Coming One. Certainly, knowledge of the historical Jesus as
well as revelations of the exalted Lord could be misused for
the glorification of man (2 Cor. 5:16; 12:1ff.); Jesus Christ
cannot be placed at man's disposal precisely because he himself is personally the exalted Lord. From one side it is correct that Paul's Christology is simultaneously soteriology.
But the "mythological" statements have a dimension beyond

121

soteriological significance. They refer to the person of
Jesus Christ himself, apart from us and also apart from preaching and church.

Pauline ethics and eschatology are treated under the general heading "Freedom" (par. 38-40). Again, this would hardly
be appropriate in a descriptive reproduction, but it makes
good sense in Bultmann's interpretation of characteristic
Pauline thought. Here the relation between the indicative and
the imperative is clarified: "freedom is the reason for demand, and the demand actualizes the freedom" (I, 336). Then
the present reality of the future life is set forth. In comparison, the concrete eschatological ideas are only fleetingly
touched upon, being really unessential. In these paragraphs
just as in earlier ones many things deserve attention, and a
few questions could be asked. However, it is not possible to
go into details.

In conclusion: I agree to a great extent with Bultmann's
interpretation of Paul's theology and gratefully acknowledge
how much I have learned from him both in years past and now in
studying his Theology of the New Testament. In general Bultmann has worked out the characteristic features of Paul's
theology very well. However, in my opinion he underestimates
the degree to which the beliefs Paul shared with the early
church remained important for him. Bultmann rightly appreci-
ates Paul's characteristic deepening interpretation and critical corrective. However, he exhibits an ultra-Pauline one-
sidedness because he isolates Paul's characteristic thought
and places it at the center of New Testament theology.

The Interpretation of Johannine Theology

The analysis of John's theology independently supports
the conclusions gained from the interpretation of Paul.. The

spiritual atmosphere of John is oriental Christianity; he de-
lineates the figure of Jesus in images from the gnostic redeemer myth. John differs from Paul by making salvation itself
rather than the way to salvation the central issue (II, 75).
Accordingly, the organization of the material must differ even
if John's theology is also interpreted existentially and to
that extent anthropologically.

Bultmann begins with "Johannine dualism." The ideas
light and darkness, life and death, etc. came from gnostic
dualism, but take on a new meaning because of John's belief in
creation. They signify the double possibility of human existence: either from God or from man himself (II, 20f.). The
dualism becomes a dualism of decision: In his decision between
faith and unfaith a man's being definitively constitutes itself,
and from then on his whence becomes clear (II, 25). Because
the world remains creation, "man's life is pervaded by the
quest for reality (alētheia), the quest for life" (II, 26).
However, because man imagines he can give himself his own answer and seeks to create security, truth is perverted into a
lie, creation into the "world." This is particularly clear in
the example of Jewish religion (II, 26-32).

The sending of the Son signifies the krisis of the world;
life appeared in the world of death for salvation and judgment.
In the person of Jesus "the transcendent divine reality became
audible, visible, and tangible in the realm of the earthly
world" (II, 33). His coming (and his departure) is the eschatological event. However, in opposition to gnosticism, it is
emphasized that the revealer is the specific historical man
Jesus of Nazareth. That is the offense of John 1:14.

How can greater precision be brought to the understanding
that the coming of Jesus is the revelation of divine reality
in the world? In order to obtain an answer to this question,

123

Bultmann follows a method of progressive reduction, excluding one element after another (II, 40ff.). Jesus is not the revealer as a mystagogue communicating teachings, formulas, and rites. Neither is he the revealer as a personality in which the divine is visible. Many passages in the Gospels portray Jesus as divine man (theios anēr), but neither his supernatural knowledge nor his miracles are what make his ministry revelatory.

His incarnation is the decisive salvation-occurrence. But death and resurrection play no role as "salvation-data" in the traditional sense; nor are the sacraments important. His words are identical with his work, but they mediate no tangible content at all save that they, as words of Jesus, are words of life, God's words. All the revelation which he brings is concentrated in the great "I am" sayings. The result of this progressive reduction is simply that Jesus, as the revealer of God, reveals nothing except that he is the revealer (II, 66).

Yet this bare fact--that he is the revealer--is not devoid of content because the revelation "is represented as the shattering and negating of all human self-assertion and all human norms and evaluations. And, precisely by virtue of being such a negation, the Revelation is the affirmation and fulfillment of human longing for life, for true reality" (II, 67f.). The way in which this is to be understood positively is worked out in the chapter "Faith" (II, 70-92). As hearing, seeing, and knowing, faith and faith alone is the way to salvation for John as well. Faith is the overcoming of the offense, deciding against the world for God. This decision of faith understands itself as a gift and has its assurance precisely in that faith in Jesus does not seek guarantees but simply hears and obeys.

In the world the believer is withdrawn from worldly existence; faith is a transition to eschatological existence. The
glory proper to faith consists in its gift of knowledge (John
17:3) and the accompanying freedom, love, joy, etc. The discussion of the relation of the indicative to the imperative is
especially important. Unlike Paul, John develops the problem
in view of the actual repeated sinning of the believer (especially in 1 John, but also in John 15). As in Paul, the relation of the indicative to the imperative is thereby understood
to be dialectical. Purity from sin is a purity extra nos, and
the imperative reminds the believer of what he already is,
thanks to the prevenient love of God encountered in the revealer (II, 80).

Apart from this last point, I have sought to develop only
the train of thought without referring to all the individual,
fruitful insights. For Bultmann's interpretation of John is
so self-consistent that its overall structure must be the
starting point for any evaluation. In distinction from his
interpretation of Paul's theology, Bultmann's analysis of
John's theology is not an overt critical interpretation.
Bultmann seems rather to assume that John himself had already
anticipated the necessary criticism of popular beliefs. Yet
even in John, Bultmann's existential approach turns out to be
a critical interpretation.

Bultmann's approach is critical first of all because he
does not base his interpretation on the canonical form of the
Gospel of John but rather on the gospel which he himself critically reconstructed in his commentary on John. There, however, the interpretation of John's theology was itself a factor contributing to the literary reconstruction. Thus, references to the sacraments, futuristic eschatology and to some
extent the framework of biblical history are eliminated. We

125

cannot discuss here the extent to which this is justified.

In the second place, Bultmann's approach is critical because he disregards the literary form of John's work: it is a
gospel, or better, a testimony (martyria, cf. John 21:24).
The narrative form is important to Bultmann only as an expression of the that of the historicity of Jesus. This interpretation is alleged to be appropriate on the grounds that John
himself has dealt very freely with the traditions of Jesus'
life (II, 127). From the perspective of the critical study of
history, this is undoubtedly an accurate observation. But
this historical perspective was completely foreign to the
fourth evangelist. Precisely for that reason it is hard to
agree that he was critically aware of his free use of tradition. Can we doubt that he accepted the facticity of what he
related, even of crude miracles? In any case, his readers in
antiquity understood what he wrote in that way, except for
Gnostics and allegorists. In other words, if I were unable to
understand what Bultmann does with John as critical interpretation, I would be forced to see it as an unwarranted modernization.

The same could be said with regard to demythologizing.
It is certainly true that the statements concerning the pre-
existence of Jesus characterize the absolute and decisive
significance of his words (II, 62). But to draw the conclusion from this that the mythological statements have lost
their mythological sense is again modern and critical; so is
the contention that Jesus is not seriously (!) presented as
"a pre-existent divine being" (II, 62).

That Jesus revealed nothing save that he is the revealer
I can only regard as a result of critical interpretation,
even though I fully recognize the intellectual power and the
logical rigor with which Bultmann has carried through his pro-

126

gressive reduction. But may one approach John with such logical criteria? It is true that in the last analysis it is the
person of Jesus that matters, and that not only the miracles
but also the "salvation-data" are meaningful only because of
their relation to him. But does it follow that they are in-
significant and superfluous? Especially with regard to the
Easter story, I find this rather dubious. The possibility of
misunderstanding (II, 45) in no way proves that for the evangelist nothing extraordinary could be visible in the history
of Jesus except for his audacious claim that God is encountered
in him (II, 49).

A thoroughgoing discussion of Bultmann's interpretation of
John would involve a detailed examination of his commentary.
Scholarship will long be occupied with it, and I will often
return with profit not only to the commentary but also to the
appropriate paragraphs of his Theology of the New Testament.
However, I cannot avoid the conclusion that in Bultmann's
existential interpretation John's theology, too, is demytholo-
gized and dehistoricized. Of course this is not to claim,
still less to prove, that the existential interpretation is
not legitimate. It is only to state my judgment that it cannot be legitimized through John's theology as it is present in
the New Testament. Thus we return again to the hermeneutical
starting point.

Concluding Remarks

Existential interpretation involves modernization. We
all modernize whenever we preach or do theology. But one must
give account for what he does; this Bultmann does consistently
and methodically. However, within New Testament scholarship
it is hazardous to modernize. Would it not be better to present as best we can New Testament thought in its full histor-

ical and mythological realism? This task is necessary and
does not preclude a personal involvement with the message of
the New Testament. But precisely for the sake of this involvement there can be no thoroughgoing separation between exegetical and theological endeavors to understand the New Testament
despite the need to distinguish them. Bultmann's existential
interpretation has arisen from painstaking attention to the
material. It is fruitful for understanding the New Testament
as his <u>Theology of the New Testament</u> proves. Yet I believe
that there is no single method which provides a normative
model.

Surely, the writings of the New Testament and what they
have to say to the present are best served when neither <u>one</u>
presentation of their theology nor <u>one</u> hermeneutical method is
alone made valid and normative. Therefore, I cannot view
Bultmann's book as <u>the</u> theology of the New Testament for our
generation. But the work is more than a rich storehouse of
exegetical observations, the mere accumulation of which merits
admiration. The work qualifies as a classic in the history of
New Testament studies. It provides an abundance of valuable
insights. The impressive synthesis as well as the many details
demand a critical involvement which cannot fail to provoke independent study of the New Testament writings. Whoever uses
it in this way will receive great profit from this book.

ESCHATOLOGY AND HISTORY IN LIGHT OF THE QUMRAN TEXTS

The Terminology

In the following remarks[1] I will use the word "eschatology" to mean doctrine of the last things, that is, statements which are concerned with events and persons of the last days. By "history" I mean socially relevant events which are the objects of reporting and research, the objects of "history" in the Greek sense.

My usage of these terms is old-fashioned. It stems from the time before Karl Barth formulated the famous sentence: "If Christianity be not altogether and unreservedly eschatology, there remains in it no relationship whatever to Christ."[2] Since that time several theologians have had a tendency to designate as eschatological anything that has anything at all to do with Christ. The meaning of the word "eschatology" has thus become so ambiguous that anyone whose native language is not German should be allowed to revert to the older usage.

Rudolf Bultmann certainly employs the word "eschatology" in such a way that its connection with history-of-religions research has been preserved. It should already be clear from my remarks on terminology, however, that it is not my intention to treat the whole problem of "history and eschatology." There are far-reaching hermeneutical, philosophical, and theological aspects to this problem as it is posed in Bultmann's Gifford Lectures.[3] At the same time, however, a definite picture of early Christianity lies at the base of Bultmann's existential interpretation.

At many points Bultmann has appropriated--perhaps too uncritically--the results of men like Wrede, Heitmüller and Bousset in order to build on the foundation they laid.[4] As

129

far as his understanding of eschatology is concerned, a connection with Albert Schweitzer seems to me quite evident. For
Bultmann, that salvation is eschatological which ends everything earthly.[5] Eschatology is thus "the doctrine of the end
of the world, of its destruction."[6] Jesus Christ is corre-
spondingly "the eschatological event, the action of God by
which God has set an end to the old world. . . The old world
has reached its end for the believer." The attitude of faith
can be designated as liberation from the world. In a paradoxical way, Christian existence is simultaneously eschatological,
unworldly, and historical.[7] But already in Albert Schweitzer
the word "eschatology" had been given a new meaning; it did
not simply signify the doctrine of the last things, but rather
an orientation of existence determined by the imminent end of
the world. "The term eschatology ought only to be applied
when reference is made to the end of the world as expected in
the immediate future, and the events, hopes, and fears connected therewith."[8] Behind Paul's expectation stands the idea
"that Jesus Christ has made an end of the natural world."[9]
When such statements are compared, it may be said that Rudolph
Bultmann has existentially interpreted Albert Schweitzer's
concept of eschatology.

By this assertion I do not of course intend that the many
profound differences between Bultmann and Schweitzer be in any
sense brushed aside as unimportant. Schweitzer was really
never a good exegete. Before him, Johannes Weiss had demonstrated by careful exegesis the eschatological nature of Jesus'
preaching concerning the kingdom of God. Basing his work on
Weiss' findings, Albert Schweitzer, with the single-mindedness
of genius, made eschatology the main key to a historical reconstruction of the life of Jesus and of the history of early
Christianity. The presuppositions for the new understanding

130

of eschatology, however, lay further in the past. They were
provided by the opening of the world of Jewish apocalyptic to
research for the first time about the middle of the last century.[10] To this extent it may be said--rather one-sidedly--
that Bultmann's work on eschatology and history stands at the
end of a period in the history of research which began when
apocalyptic literature came to light.

The Importance of the Qumran Texts

To a certain extent research today is in a situation similar to that of a century ago. New source material for the
history of Judaism and its eschatology has become accessible
to us but has only partially been evaluated scientifically and
theologically. In order to assess and evaluate correctly the
material stemming from the caves near Qumran it seems appropriate to me to work with a terminology which is least bur-
dened by present-day debates. Thus my old-fashioned usage of
terms.

The new material cannot easily be fitted into the picture
we have of Jewish eschatology. From Baldensperger to Mowinckel,[11] to mention only two names, a distinction has been made
between a national expectation of the future which is concerned
with this world, and an apocalyptic expectation which is univer-
salistic and transcendental. The Davidic Messiah is said to
belong to the former inner-Jewish movement; to the latter belongs the heavenly Son of Man which is influenced by Iranian
religion. In the Qumran writings we find a dualistic doctrine
of two spirits, the prince of light and the angel of darkness,
who oppose each other from creation to the end of the world.
An apocalyptic, super-human messianic figure, however, in no
way corresponds to this speculative doctrine. No trace can be
found of the Son of Man. Rather, the eschatological persons

131

named in the Qumran writings are officeholders within the
Israel of the last days.

But the two conceptions, the dualistic and the messianic,
are not simply juxtaposed. The dualism receives its concrete
form as a dualism between the sons of light and the sons of
darkness, that is--in practice--between the members of the
sect and its adversaries. The eschatological officeholders
exercise their functions in the predestined final confronta-
tion between the two groups. It is therefore permissible to
elucidate the relationship between eschatology and history by
means of the statements concerning these persons. There is
all the more reason to do so since in the New Testament, eschatology and history converge above all in Christology.

The views of scholars vary widely concerning the importance of the Qumran findings for the historical understanding
of the beginnings of Christology. A. Dupont-Sommer has interpreted the so-called "Teacher of Righteousness" as a Christ-
figure prior to Christ. Others have attempted to explain the
Christology of Hebrews or even the use of the title Christ in
the Synoptics from the perspective of the Qumran doctrine regarding the priestly Messiah.[12] On the other hand, it has
been maintained, one might even say apodictically, that the
Qumran texts are thoroughly unproductive for understanding the
Christology of the early church.[13] This judgment, in my opinion, rests on sounder exegesis and sharper critical discrimi-
nation. Nevertheless, the purely negative assessment is not
the last word on the subject. Today we must move beyond a
direct comparison of isolated texts and concepts to a more
structural approach. Krister Stendahl, for example, has
emphasized this.[14] But Bultmann saw this as well when he
found the most important analogy in the fact that the early
Christian community, precisely as the Qumran sect, understood

132

itself as the true Israel of the last days.[15]

Formerly, we had on the one hand a Jewish eschatological
body of writings which were often difficult to date. We knew
little about the historical-sociological background of its
statements and ideas. On the other hand, above all in Josephus, we had a whole list of reports and notes about freedom-
fighters and charismatics from the time of Judas Maccabaeus
to Simon bar Kochba. However, the sources were almost completely silent regarding the basis for the eschatological expectations, the claims of the leading figures, and the way
these expectations and claims were developed by interpretation
of Scripture.

The findings at Qumran have placed us in a new position.
Our picture of the messianic ideas of pre-Christian Judaism is
being enlarged and corrected. The necessity of relating and
comparing the Qumran material with Jewish conceptions attested
elsewhere frees us from our in-born tendency to examine too
hastily and uncritically Jewish messianic ideas for their relationships to Christology. It is of great importance that we
are now quite well-informed about the eschatological doctrines
as well as about the sociological structures and history of
one and the same movement. This means that it has now become
possible to study the relationship between eschatology and
history within one community which was close to Jesus and to
the early church both in time and in location. It can to
some extent be demonstrated how history was interpreted in
light of eschatology and on the other hand how traditional
eschatology was transformed under the impact of history.

Persons Expected to Come

In the Scroll of the Rule, at the end of a series of
legal prescriptions, it says: "And they shall be governed by

133

the first ordinances in which the members of the Community began their instruction, until the coming of the Prophet and the Anointed [ones] of Aaron and Israel."[16] According to this the legal ordinances are understood as interim laws which may not be altered during the pre-eschatological period. A similar mode of expression occurs several times in the Damascus Document.[17] It is known, however, from other sources as well:

"Until a trustworthy prophet should arise" (1 Macc. 14:41; (cf. 4:46).

"Until a [the] priest with Urim and Thummim should arise" (Neh. 7:65; Ezra 2:63).

"Until he comes whose right it is" (Ezek. 21:27).

One may also compare the messianically interpreted oracle concerning Judah in Genesis 49:10: "Until he comes to whom it belongs." According to the exegesis of the inhabitants of Qumran still another passage is included, Hosea 10:12, which was understood as "until he comes and teaches you righteousness" or "until the coming of the Teacher of Righteousness" (cf. CD vi, 11). In talmudic and post-talmudic literature, this text was applied to the return of Elijah.[18]

The eschatological interpretation of these biblical passages noted belonged in all probability to common Jewish exegetical tradition. However, in the text from the Rule (IQS 9:10f.), a Prophet, a royal, and a priestly Messiah are mentioned alongside one another. It has long been recognized that three figures are intended, and this has been subsequently confirmed by the citation of Deuteronomy 18:18ff.,[19] Numbers 24:15-17, and Deuteronomy 33:8-11 in a collection of testimonies.[20] We may not interpret these texts in light of a Christian conception of precursors of the Messiah. We have to do here with three contemporaneous eschatological officeholders.[21] One may probably see in the emphatic differentiation between the three offices a polemical allusion directed against their

134

combination by the Hasmonean priest-princes. It is said of
John Hyrcanus that he combined a prophetic gift with the sovereign and high-priestly offices.[22]

The expectation of all three figures was based on Holy
Scripture; the scriptural bases, however, are employed quite
differently in the three cases. Of the prophet we actually
learn nothing beyond the fact that the prediction of the
"prophet like Moses" was applied to him.[23] Among the Samari-
tans and perhaps in other circles he stood in the center of
expectation. Yet in later "normative" Judaism the prophet as
an independent eschatological figure has vanished. Perhaps
for the enthusiasts the temptation was too great to play the
role of the prophet.

What is said in the Qumran texts about the Davidic Messiah, the anointed one of Israel, is almost exclusively a paraphrase and interpretation of well-known messianic prophecies:
Genesis 49:8-12; Numbers 24:15-17; Isaiah 11, etc.[24] Of particular interest is the clear proof that the promise of Nathan
in 2 Samuel 7 was interpreted messianically in pre-Christian
Judaism. This text must have had great significance for the
beginnings of Christology as well as for the emergence and
development of the entire expectation of the Messiah. The
Rabbis, however, avoid the text, apparently because it could
serve as a basis for the doctrine of Christ as the Son of God.[25]

The image of the Davidic Messiah in the Qumran texts is in
essential agreement with the traditional picture, cf. for example Ps. Sol. 17. But it has been modified. In connection with
the priestly-theocratic conceptions once held by Ezekiel, the
offspring of David is not called king, but "prince of the community." At the assembly, at the sacred meal, and even in the
war of the last days he is associated with and even subordi-
nated to the eschatological high priest.[26] This ordering

reflects the community's structure.

The expectation of an Aaronic high priest in the last days in all probability must also have belonged to the old stock of eschatological ideas. It could be deduced from Zechariah (chapters 2, 4, and 6) as well as from Jeremiah (33:17-22) that in the last days a Levitical priest would stand beside the Davidic ruler. Several texts could be applied to the eschatological high priest: the oracle concerning Levi in Deuteronomy 33:8-11, the promise to Phinehas of a perpetual priesthood in Numbers 25:11-13, and the saying concerning God's covenant with Levi in Malachi 2:4-8. This can be confirmed by rabbinic sources, although there the high priest of the last days remains a rather stereotyped figure.[27] It is strange however that in the Qumran writings these Old Testament texts are little used. Yet the functions of the high priest are quite thoroughly described.[28] The actual cultic service, however, with its sacrifice and expiation rites is less emphasized than the coming high priest's commission to offer prayers and thanksgivings in the assembly, at the common meal, and in the holy war, as well as to give instruction from Scripture concerning the will of God. In other words, the picture of the messianic prince is traditional but that of the high priest is to a great extent an image projected into the future for which the activity of a leading priest within the Qumran community served as a model.

In the case of the historical Teacher of Righteousness, the relationship to the words of Scripture is of a different sort. His name comes from the passage already cited, Hosea 10:12 (cf. also Joel 2:23). In the Qumran writings these texts are not cited, however. Instead, a whole list of passages from the prophets and the Psalms is applied to the Teacher and his opponents. Evidently these texts were not

traditionally understood as statements regarding the coming
Teacher of Righteousness. Rather, they were cited because
they could be interpreted ex eventu as prophecies of the appearance and fate of the founder of the community designated
by this title.[29] The historical Teacher was understood as the
one who fulfilled the hope for a coming moreh sedek, and in
light of his fate many texts were reinterpreted as prophecies
pertaining to him.

Critical examination of the texts yields no reliable basis
for the hypothesis that the return of the historical Teacher in
the form of a priestly Messiah was expected.[30] Nevertheless,
these two figures have several features in common. Both have
the same names: "the priest," "Interpreter of the Torah,"
"teacher of righteousness."[31] To a great extent they share
the same functions: teaching, interpretation of Scripture,
prayer, thanksgiving, and leadership of the community.[32] Accordingly, one may not speak of an identity of persons but of
an identity of office.[33] The difference between the two is
that the historical Teacher exercised his function at a time
of eschatological tribulations, while the messianic high
priest will officiate at a time of eschatological war and salvation. The conclusion may be drawn that the images of the
historical Teacher and the eschatological high priest have
influenced one another.

Some scholars have conjectured that the Teacher was identified with the eschatological prophet.[34] There is, however,
no textual basis for this hypothesis. It is probably understandable that the expectation of the prophet grew weaker, for
actually there remained no special function for him. The task
of a prophet in this environment must have been principally
inspired interpretation of Scripture and legal instruction,
and these tasks came to be assigned to the historical teacher

and the eschatological priest.

But there is another hypothesis that warrants careful consideration, namely, that during his lifetime the teacher was regarded as a candidate for the high-priestly office and to this extent was an Aaronic _Messias designatus_.[35] This could explain a number of things. Admittedly, difficult historical problems remain (Was the _moreh sedek_ a legitimate Zadokite?) as well as exegetical problems, above all in the interpretation of the Damascus Document.[36]

Within this movement, which we may call Essene, eschatological conceptions were altered. What united the members of the communities in Judaism and distinguished them from other groups was much more the legal ordering of life than theological doctrines.[37] In the Damascus Document, one Messiah of Aaron and Israel has developed from the two anointed ones of Aaron and Israel. The singular may no longer be regarded as a scribal error in the medieval manuscript from the Cairo Geniza since it has been attested in a fragment from Cave IV.[38] The reformulation of eschatology has to do with a change in the sociological structure. In the Damascus Document a division within the leadership of the community also appears to be lacking. The designation priests, Levites, and sons of Zadok are applied by means of spiritualizing exegesis to the first generation of the movement, its adherents, and the elect at the end of days.[39] In the messianic doctrine the duality of the priestly and princely offices is dropped. What is emphasized is rather the chronological duality, of the former Teacher and the coming Messiah of Aaron and Israel, who is probably called both "prince of the whole congregation" and "he who teaches righteousness."[40] This change may also have something to do with a cessation of hostility against the Hasmonean princes in the particular branch of the movement which is represented in

the Damascus Document. Nothing is said here about the oppo-
nent of the legitimate Teacher.

The Interrelationship of History and Eschatology

Much more could be said of course about the interpretation of texts and historical details. I am only interested,
however, in what is illustrated by the details, namely, the
correlation between the sociological structure and history of
the communities and their eschatological interpretation of
Scripture and messianic doctrine. Events and persons are
understood in light of eschatological prophecies, and transmitted texts and concepts receive new explanations from events.
Interpretations and reinterpretations are not merely subsequent
additions; eschatological interpretations and reinterpretations
must already have been formative factors in the events themselves.

The process of interpretation and reinterpretation, of
historicizing and eschatologizing, was definitely not something peculiar to the Essenes. Similar things occurred again
and again. At the beginning of messianic doctrine there already exists royal ideology as well as the peculiar history of
David. It was probably expected of many a king of Judah that
he would be a new David and by God's grace a king of salvation.
But hopes were disappointed and projected further into the
future. Deutero-Isaiah actualized these eschatological expectations. His prophecies were partially fulfilled; however,
they achieved their lasting significance as promises for a
more distant future. What Haggai and Zechariah prophesied
concerning the Davidic Zerubbabel and the high priest Joshua
became the basis for the doctrine of the two anointed ones.
In the Book of Daniel, old traditions are applied to the present and to the immediate future. Afterward Daniel provided

139

the basis for all apocalyptic. We may not speak of eschatology in the case of the Maccabees if we associate the idea of
the end of the world with it. Nevertheless, this time was
seen as one of fulfilled promises.[41] The Hasmonean priest-
princes appear to have substituted for the legitimacy they
lacked the assertion that because of their zeal for God their
family was the genuine spiritual descendent of Phinehas.[42]
With numerous variations, the same pattern must have been repeated in Zealot movements. The expectation of a Messiah ben
Ephraim who falls in war is rooted in Scripture; but it reflects the fate of the leaders in the wars of independence,
above all that of Bar Kochba.[43]

How completely it was possible for eschatological interpretation of Scripture to be bent in light of real events becomes strikingly clear in Josephus, who was able to apply the
saying concerning the world ruler who would arise from Judah
(Gen. 49:10?) to Vespasian.[44] An example from a much later
period is the story of Sabbatai Zevi who during imprisonment
was converted to Islam. This led to the development of a
doctrine of the necessity for apostasy by the Messiah. In this
story Gershom Scholem has seen the most interesting parallel
to the Christian doctrine of the crucified Messiah--from the
Jewish standpoint.[45]

The writings from the Dead Sea caves are thus suited to
sharpen our picture of the complexity of the Jewish doctrines
concerning eschatological persons. The result of our brief
overview may be stated as follows: The correlation between
eschatology and history is by no means exclusively Christian
or peculiar to the New Testament. Rather, expectations are
repeatedly applied anew to the present situation, and the
eschatological texts and conceptions have undergone constant
reinterpretation. Expectation of the imminent end, realized

eschatology, eschatology in the process of realization, proleptic and inaugurated eschatology--all of these can be found,
mutatis mutandis, in Judaism as well. The problem of the delay of the awaited end was only too familiar.[46]

What is new and unique with respect to Jesus is not the
belief that the end and salvation are at hand or already present. Interest is not confined here to the mere "that"; of
decisive importance are the "what," "how," and "who." Actual
events, interpretation of Scripture, and eschatology are interwoven in early Christianity in approximately the same way they
were in the Qumran writings and in other branches of Judaism.
But in the New Testament everything is altered because concern
is focused on new and different events, in a phrase, on the
name "Jesus Christ" which is simultaneously a historical and
an eschatological name.

Summary -- A Working Hypothesis

The actual form of the relationship in the New Testament
between historical event, eschatological doctrine and reinterpretation of Scripture can only be made clear by detailed and
penetrating studies. Yet I may be permitted briefly to sketch
what I regard as working hypotheses.

1. The transference of the title Messiah to Jesus and
the new meaning it received as a name of Jesus can be explained
neither from the Jewish concept of the Messiah, nor from the
preaching of Jesus, nor from belief in the resurrection as
such. What was decisive was rather the historical fact that
Jesus was accused as a messianic pretender and was executed as
"King of the Jews."[47] This brutal fact led the early church to
christologically reinterpret messianic texts and to read as
messianic predictions texts not applied to the Messiah in Judaism.

141

2. The Easter events were for the disciples unexpected occurrences, yet occurrences which nevertheless took place. They were something to be interpreted; they were not themselves an interpretation of the significance of Jesus and his death.[48] The Easter events were interpreted with reference to the eschatological hope of the resurrection and the testimony of Scripture, again in quite diverse ways. All of eschatology had to be newly explained in light of the resurrection of Jesus Christ which had already occurred, and indeed in a way unforeseen in Judaism.

3. The events of Jesus' death and resurrection led to a heightening of eschatological anticipation.[49] Paul's varied usage of the formula "until so-and-so comes" may serve as an illustration. The one who is to come is identified with the one who died for us. In the interim the concern surpasses mere adherence to the legal formulations of a teacher: while giving thanks, the bread is broken and the cup is blessed in remembrance of Jesus, and thus the Lord's death is proclaimed "until he comes" (1 Cor. 11:26). But eschatological formulas can also be applied to the earthly appearance of Jesus in such a way that the Mosaic law itself is regarded as an interim decree: it was added for the sake of transgressions "until the offspring should come to whom the promise has been made" (Gal. 3:19).[50]

4. The appearance of the early Christian expectation of the parousia also belongs to the transformation of eschatology in light of history. In Judaism men awaited the coming of the eschatological officeholders and, connected with that, the Messiah's assumption of power; some groups may have hoped for the heavenly enthronement of the Son of Man.[51] The idea of the parousia of the Savior in the sense of his coming from heaven to earth at the end of time, however, can hardly be

142

attested in Jewish sources. In contrast, by its very nature
the early Christian expectation of the parousia is the hope
that the One who had already been on earth would come from
heaven in power and splendor. Thus we may not begin with the
expectation of the parousia and of the impending end of the
world in such a way that the delay of the parousia becomes the
main problem in early Christian eschatology.[52]

5. In contrast to what often occurred in Judaism, the
eschatological expectations that had been actualized through
Jesus were not subsequently detached from his person to be
bound up in altered form with new historical figures. As far
as salvation figures were concerned, the constantly changing
correlation between eschatology and history came to an end in
the christological confession. Only the expectation of the
parousia could be revitalized again and again by historical
events, as happened often already during New Testament times.
Thus more radically than in Judaism, the Christian doctrine
concerning the last things became a doctrine of the end of the
world and of history.

6. With some variation in details, the New Testament
transformation of eschatology is characterized by the tendency to relate all promises to Jesus (cf. 2 Cor. 1:20!).
Texts and titles which in Judaism had been distributed among
various eschatological (and non-eschatological) figures all
served to attest the honor and significance of the one Christ.
The concentration of the expectation upon Jesus, and the accumulation of all titles and testimonies associated with it,
cannot be explained by the brute facts of the crucifixion and
of the resurrection of Jesus. The presupposition for this
concentration is rather the person and appearance of the
earthly Jesus--even if he himself never laid claim to messianic dignity. No existing messianic category was adequate to

him, yet he appeared with such authority that all the hopes
of the disciples focused on him.

7. What forms the central theme of biblical eschatology
is not so much the end of the world and of history as the fulfillment of God's promises.[53] For the New Testament, Jesus
Christ is an eschatological figure, and the events connected
with his name are eschatological principally because through
him the promises of God are fulfilled. In a historical description of New Testament theology, therefore, history of
interpretation must receive its due.[54] This does not mean,
of course, that New Testament Christology can be understood
simply in light of the Old Testament. The Old Testament texts
were available to the early Christians as they had already
been interpreted in Judaism. Hellenistic and Gnostic influ-
ences as well are not to be excluded. Exegesis was--then as
always--the means whereby contemporary ideas could be connected with sacred texts and traditions. But above all we must
observe that all texts and titles, concepts and myths which
contributed to the interpretation of the history of Jesus were
reinterpreted in the light of the event.

My attempt to shed new light on the relationship between
eschatology and history from the Qumran texts has in a certain
sense turned from the modern question concerning time, history,
and eschatology back to the old schema, "promise and fulfillment." The theological problems have hardly been simplified,
for the old doctrine of prophecy and fulfillment can no longer
be reproduced in its classic form. It has become only too
clear to us to what a great extent fulfillment always involves
a reinterpretation of the promise; only in that way can it be
understood as fulfillment.[55]

Behind Bultmann's work on the theme "history and eschatology" lies not only knowledge of history, but also a herme-

neutical program and a theological stance. My goal was much
more modest; I wanted simply to make a few historical observations on the theme. Yet if it is correct that Bultmann's view
has in part been determined by a definite epoch of the history
of research within New Testament studies, discussion with him
may be carried on not only on the philosophical, hermeneutical
and theological levels. We must begin again and again with
exegetical and historical study, conscious that it may be a
long time before historical-critical analysis and theological
interpretation are again brought together in as impressive a
synthesis as Bultmann's.

THE ATONEMENT--AN ADEQUATE REWARD FOR THE AKEDAH?

By the Atonement I here understand the death of Jesus interpreted as a divine act of redemption, regardless of the specific terminology used by various writers. The Akedah means
what in Christian tradition is called the sacrifice and in
Jewish tradition the binding of Isaac (ʾakēdat yishāk), as
interpreted in the Aggadah. Similarities between the atonement and the Akedah have long been observed. Modern discussion of the relationship between the two traditions started
when Isidore Lévi in 1912 argued for the independence and
priority of the Jewish lore.[1] The immediate reaction was
slight, but after World War II the theme was taken up by a
number of scholars, including H. J. Schoeps,[2] H. Riesenfeld,[3]
and E. R. Goodenough.[4] A brilliant analysis of Akedah traditions up to the twelfth century C.E. has been presented by S.
Spiegel, originally published in Hebrew and recently translated into English by Judah Goldin, whose Introduction conveys
important insights into the general nature of aggadic interpretation.[5] Later studies by G. Vermes[6] and R. Le Déaut[7] have
concentrated upon early traditions, with special attention
paid to the various versions of the Palestinian Targum. Even
patristic and iconographic materials have been gathered.[8]

It may be assumed that the most relevant sources have
been fairly well exhausted by these studies. Lévi's presentation has been supplemented and modified at a number of points,
but his main thesis concerning the independence of the Jewish
tradition has been confirmed. Reactions to the Christian doctrine of the atonement may have stimulated the development of
the Aggadah, but only as a secondary factor. Much more open
is the other problem, namely, to what extent and in which ways

the Akedah served as a model for early Christian understanding
of the atonement. The number of parallels would be hard to
explain without the assumption of some kind of relationship,
and yet the New Testament texts are elusive. The few explicit
references to the sacrifice of Isaac do not deal with the
atonement,[9] and passages that deal with the atonement may be
more or less reminiscent of the Akedah but never make the
allusion explicit.[10] This is the case even in Romans 8:32
where the formulation, "He who did not spare his own Son but
gave him up for us all," is obviously reminiscent of Genesis
22, as has been recognized by exegetes from Origen onward.[11]
Why did Paul use a phrase drawn from the story of Abraham's
sacrifice of his son in order to speak about the death of
Christ? An answer to this question would illuminate the way
in which the atonement was first related to the Akedah. The
results may remain conjectural, but an exploration is worth
attempting.

In Romans 8:32 the allusion is unambiguous, but Paul in
no way draws it to the attention of his readers. They might
perfectly well understand what he had to say in this context
without being aware of the biblical phraseology. In fact, a
number of commentators pass it over in silence.[12] If the allusion is recognized, it may simply call for an emotional response: No gift can be greater than that of Abraham, who did
not withhold his only son! One can hardly object when C. K.
Barrett notes the allusion but writes, "Paul makes no serious
use of it."[13] Adolf Jülicher even issued a warning: "The
words of the poet do not provide materials for critical exer-
cises."[14] Yet, research starts with curiosity, and I wonder
whether there might not be more behind the biblical phraseology than what is apparent in the context of Paul's letter.

The form of Romans 8:32 is that of a syllogism; if the

protasis is valid, the apodosis cannot but follow. Within its
present context, the passage reminiscent of Abraham's sacrifice
therefore functions as a warrant for the certitude of full salvation. As to its content, the passage runs parallel to Romans
5:8-9 and 5:10, where we have the more regular form for a conclusion a fortiori, with <u>pollō</u> <u>mallon</u>.[15] The formulations are
open to variation, but Paul can assume that there is agreement
upon the protasis and, quite likely, that such formulations
were familiar to Christians at Rome. The same holds true also
for the famous <u>hilastērion</u>-passage in Romans 3:24-26, to which
the other passages on the atonement refer back. In general,
while Paul drew new and radical consequences, his basic affir-
mations concerning the person of Christ and the event of atonement conform to accepted statements of kerygma, creed, and
liturgy.[16]

In his commentary on Romans, O. Michel has argued that
Romans 8:32a is based upon some fixed form of preaching.[17] He
finds the use of first person plural to be typical for the
style of confession and points to the creed-like relative
clauses in v. 34 as well as to the analogous passages in Romans
4:25 and John 3:16. Even the linguistic form favours the assumption that Paul's formulation is based upon tradition.
Whereas <u>ouk</u> <u>epheisato</u> corresponds to the Septuagint, <u>tou</u> <u>idiou</u>
<u>huiou</u> does not, but is rather an independent rendering of the
Hebrew text.[18] Paul is likely to have commented upon the traditional formula not only by appending the apodosis but also
by adding <u>pantōn</u> to the current phrase <u>hyper</u> <u>hēmōn</u> in the
protasis. Thus he stresses a main theme of his letter, at the
same time achieving a rhetorical correspondence between <u>hyper</u>
<u>hēmōn</u> <u>pantōn</u> and <u>ta</u> <u>panta</u> <u>hēmin</u>. The latter phrase probably
refers to nothing short of the eschatological inheritance
promised to Abraham and his offspring.[19] Persons familiar

with the Genesis texts and their early Christian interpretation may have realized that Paul's cryptic allusion indicated the possibility of scriptural backing for what he wrote.

If Paul's formulation in Romans 8:32a is not created ad hoc, it is no longer sufficient to assume a loose and not very serious use of biblical phraseology. In recent years a number of scholars, representing various schools, have proved that the New Testament use of Scripture presupposes much more conscientious exegetical work than we were formerly inclined to think.[20] The formulation in Romans 8:32a is likely to go back to some kind of midrashic interpretation. The exegetical pattern can hardly have been other than one of correspondence: as Abraham did not spare his son, so God did not spare his own Son. The question is how this correspondence was understood. According to a predominant, now somewhat fading, mood one would immediately think of the analogy between type and antitype. And certainly it was possible to find a typological relationship between the "binding of Isaac" and the death of Christ.[21] But typology cannot be made the general principle of early Christian hermeneutics, and the statement in Romans 8:32a relates to the conduct of Abraham and not to the suffering of Isaac. It is unlikely that Abraham's act of obedience was ever considered a typological prefiguration of God's act of love.[22]

The text of Genesis 22:16-17 suggests a different type of correspondence, that of act and reward. "By myself I have sworn, says the Lord, because you have done this, and have not withheld your son, your only son, I will indeed bless you," etc. A homiletic exposition or paraphrase of this may well have been the original context of the passage now found in Romans 8:32a. God rewarded Abraham by a corresponding action, not sparing his own Son, but giving him up for us (i.e. the descendants of Abraham), and thus he indeed blessed Abraham and made all nations be blessed in his offspring. A homiletic interpretation of this type is not a pure construction. It is attested by Irenaeus: "For Abraham, according to his faith, followed the commandment of the Word of God, and with ready mind gave up his only and beloved son, as a sacrifice to God, in order that God might be pleased to offer His beloved and only Son for all his offspring, as a sacrifice for our salvation."[23] In the Armenian version the idea of reward is even more explicit; it speaks of Abraham as the one "who also through faith asked God that for the sake of humanity (=philanthropy?) He might reward him for his son."[24] The language used is not derived from Romans 8:32 and the reference to Abraham's offspring points to a Jewish-Christian origin of the paraphrase. Is it conceivable that Irenaeus cites a later version of the "Aggadah" from which already Romans 8:32a was drawn?[25]

The passage in Irenaeus does not provide more than late and therefore uncertain evidence in favour of a conjecture which I would have dared to venture even without it: the allusion to Genesis 22 in Romans 8:32a is best explained on the assumption that it is derived from an exposition in which the atonement was understood as an "adequate reward" for the Akedah. Obviously, the adequacy should not be understood in terms of quantitative equivalence but as an exact correspondence of quality. In fact, this is how the rule "measure for measure" was applied both in Judaism and in early Christianity.[26] Some early Jewish adherent of the crucified Messiah may have taken Genesis 22 to imply that God, who judges those who judge and shows mercy upon those who act with mercy, rewarded Abraham's sacrifice by offering up his own Son. If this view was actually held, it would provide a most satisfactory explanation for Paul's otherwise cryptic reference in

150

Romans 8:32. Caution forbids us to postulate that Paul's statement may not be explained otherwise. The conjecture would, however, gain in probability if it can be proved: (1) that the understanding of the atonement as a reward for the Akedah conforms to some trend in contemporary Aggadah, (2) that the hypothesis is supported rather than contradicted by other evidence in Paul's letters, and (3) that it would be in harmony with our general knowledge of pre-Pauline Jewish Christianity. In all three respects I regard the evidence as favourable to the conjecture.

I

In Jewish traditions, Isaac was early regarded as a model for suffering martyrs,[27] but there is little, if any, evidence that he was ever seen as a prototype of the Messiah.[28] In several texts, however, God is said to remember the Akedah and therefore to rescue the descendants of Isaac on various occasions, from the Exodus to the resurrection of the dead.[29] Both the daily sacrifices in the temple and the blowing of the Shofar at Rosh ha-Shanah are said to make God recall the Akedah.[30] References in prayers offer features of special interest. The kernel of the tradition may be a simple prayer that God might remember the binding of Isaac to the benefit of Israel.[31] But in various ways this was spelled out in terms of an "adequate reward." In the Palestinian Targums a prayer is attributed to Abraham, with the following conclusion: "I have done Thy word with joy and have effected Thy decree. And now, when his (Isaac's) children come into a time of distress ('aktā), remember the binding ('ªkedāh) of Isaac, their father, and listen to their prayer, and answer them and deliver them from all distress."[32] Here the point of correspondence is that God might listen to Israel's prayers, as Abraham listened to God's word.

A version of the Aggadah on the prayer of the patriarch, attributed to Rabbi Johanan, includes a reference to Genesis 21:12, "Through Isaac shall your descendants be named." When God, in spite of this promise, told Abraham to offer Isaac as a burnt offering, he could have made a retort. But he suppressed his impulse and asked God to act likewise: "Whenever Isaac's children enter into distress, and there is no one to act as their advocate, do Thou speak up as their advocate."[33] That is, as Abraham made no retort, so God should make no retort. Another variation of the motif is found in the Zikronoth, part of the additional prayer for Rosh ha-Shanah: "Consider (lit. may there appear before Thee) the binding with which Abraham our Father bound his son Isaac on the altar, suppressing his compassion in order to do Thy will. So let Thy compassion suppress Thine anger (and remove it) from us."[34] It is not necessary here to discuss the relationship between legends and liturgy or to mention all variants. What is important may best be summarized in Spiegel's statement: "It may be surmised that all these variations originally had one feature in common: a parallelism between Abraham's conduct at the Akedah and the conduct expected in return from God."[35]

The parallelism is also attested outside the Akedah prayers. Already R. Benaiah, third generation Tannaite, said that at the Exodus the waters were cleft because Abraham cleaved the wood.[36] From later sources we hear similar comments: "As Abraham bound his son below, so the Holy One, blessed be He, tied the princes of the pagans above."[37] Due to Abraham's worship the descendants of Isaac were found worthy to worship at Mount Sinai and the exiles will be reassembled to worship in Jerusalem.[38] "On the third day" the dead will be raised up because of the "third day" of Father Abraham.[39] His ten trials were rewarded by the

152

ten plagues in Egypt, and they may serve as a compensation when the ten commandments are broken.[40] The playfulness of such interpretations should not be overlooked, nor should the basic principle of "adequate reward." The same principle can also be applied to other chapters of Abraham's story, as in a homily on Genesis 18 where it is explicitly stated: "'And the Lord went before them by day' (Exod. 13:21). This is to teach you that with what measure a man metes, it is meted out to him. Abraham accompanied the ministering angels ... (Gen. 18:16), and God accompanied his children in the wilderness. ... (Exod. 13:21)." A similar correspondence is found with regard to supply of water, bread, and meat, shelter, and attendance and protection.[41]

None of this material is older than Paul, but all of it illustrates a tendency, well established in the tannaitic period, to relate the history of Israel to the story of Abraham, including the Akedah, by application of the principle "measure for measure." Yet at the crucial point, Abraham's offering of his son, the principle was not applied in non-Christian Judaism. Only an interpreter who believed the crucified Jesus to be Messiah and Son of God could dare to follow the trend consistently to its bitter end, saying that as Abraham offered up his son, so God offered up His own son for Isaac's children.

II

Apart from Romans 8:32 the clearest Pauline allusion to Genesis 22 is found in Galatians 3:13-14. V. 14a, "That the blessing of Abraham might come upon the Gentiles," is a paraphrase of Genesis 22:18, "And in your offspring shall all the nations of the earth be blessed." The expression "the blessing of Abraham" is taken from Genesis 28:4, and "in Christ Jesus" has been substituted for "in your offspring."[42] It is

153

also likely that the notion of substitution in v. 13 is related to Genesis 22. Here too there is a conscientious interpretation in the background. In Deuteronomy 21:23 it was stated that a hanged man was accursed. This might be taken to exclude faith in a crucified Messiah, but the passage could be turned into an argument in favour of the Christian faith if "a man hanging upon a tree" was combined with "a ram caught in a thicket" (Gen. 22:13). Thus the crucified Jesus was understood to be the lamb of sacrifice provided by God. Here there is an element of typology; but the ram, rather than Isaac, is seen as a type of Christ.

The allusions to Genesis 22 in Galatians 3 are all contained in vv. 13a-14. These verses must be a fragment of pre-Pauline tradition. By his comment in v. 14b Paul identifies the blessing of Abraham with the Spirit, given as a down-payment even to Gentile believers. Thus he makes the fragment bear upon the Galatian controversy, but blurs the distinction between "us," the Israelites, and the Gentile nations. Moreover, Paul interprets redemption from the curse of the Law to imply freedom from the Law itself. But the phrase, "Christ redeemed us from the curse of the Law," by itself suggests no more than liberation from the curse inflicted by transgressions of the Law, in analogy with Daniel 9:11. According to the pre-Pauline tradition the Messiah, through his substitutionary death upon the cross, redeemed the Israelites from the curse caused by their transgressions. As a consequence of Israel's redemption the blessing of Abraham would come upon the Gentiles in Abraham's offspring, the Messiah Jesus. The fragment must be of Jewish-Christian origin. Most likely it is derived from a "midrash" on Genesis 22.

Without considering possible connections with the Akedah a number of scholars have argued that Paul makes use of tradi-

tional formulations in Romans 3:24-25.[43] Others have found
that the passage alludes to Genesis 22:8, "God will Himself
provide the lamb for a burnt offering."[44] It is philologically
possible to translate hon proetheto ho theos hilastērion as
"whom God appointed (designed, purposed) to be an expiation."[45]
There is some difficulty in that we have no evidence protithes-
thai was ever used to render yir'eh, Genesis 22:8, or the y r'h
of 22:14.[46] But the twofold theory, that Paul cites a tradition of Jewish-Christian origin in which the atonement was related to the Akedah, would help explain several features in the
text of Romans 3:24-26. The use of the term hilastērion has
its closest analogy in dia ... tou hilastēriou (tou) thanatou
autōn, 4 Maccabees 17:22, where the vicarious death of the
Maccabean martyrs is seen as an imitation of Isaac. The blood
of Isaac is mentioned in early traditions, and redemption,
mostly the prototypical redemption from Egypt, is related to
the Akedah.[47] The phrase en Christō Iēsou may well be of pre-
Pauline origin on the assumption that "in Christ Jesus" is a
paraphrase of "in your offspring," as in Galatians 3:14a.[48]

Considerable problems have been caused by the phrase dia
tēn paresin tōn progegonotōn hamartēmatōn. This has often been
taken to mean God's tolerant "passing over" sins in the past,
but a number of exegetes take paresis as a synonym for aphesis.
They mostly assume that dia with accusative is in the sense of
dia with genitive. Thus, the clause would state that God's
righteousness was manifested through the forgiveness of past
sins. The rare word paresis is, however, attested to mean
legal non-prosecution, dropping of a case.[49] There is no reason why it should not be used in the same sense in Romans 3:25.
The sins were committed in the past, in the generations between
Isaac and Christ. That the prosecution was dropped, however,
is the negative counter-part of providing for expiation and

155

does not refer to tolerance in the past. The following translation may be proposed: "Whom God designed to be an expiation
... by his blood, in order to manifest his righteousness, because the prosecution of the sins committed in the past was
dropped in the forbearance of God, so that his righteousness
might be manifested in the present time."[50] This interpretation is favoured by the analogy with Romans 8:31ff. There the
allusion to the Akedah is followed by the question, "Who shall
bring any charge against God's elect?" As God, who did not
spare his own Son, is the one who justifies, the case has been
dropped, and there will be no prosecution. Somewhat analogous
also are the Akedah prayers in which God is asked not to make
any retort to the children of Isaac or not to listen to their
accusers, but to speak up as their advocate.[51]

Along this line of interpretation also the meaning of the
clause eis endeiksin tēs dikaiosynēs autou becomes clear. It
does not refer to a justice that requires either punishment or
expiation, or to righteousness as a gift of God, or simply to
God's covenantal faithfulness.[52] The phrase is best understood
in analogy with Romans 3:4f., "That thou mayest be justified in
thy words," etc. Providing for an expiation, God manifested
his righteousness, i.e., he vindicated himself as being righteous and doing what he had said.[53] This he did in spite of
Israel's sins in the past, because in divine forbearance he
dropped the charge against them. In the original context of
the fragment it would have been clear that the manifestation
of God's righteousness implied, quite especially, that he kept
his oath to Abraham (Gen. 22:16-18). Thus, the fragments of
ancient tradition preserved in Romans 8:32, Galatians 3:13-14,
and Romans 3:25f., concur not merely by using a phraseology
vaguely reminiscent of the Akedah but also in interpreting the
atonement as the fulfilment of what God promised by a solemn

oath to Abraham after the sacrifice of Isaac.[54]

In the Pauline Epistles all passages reminiscent of the Akedah seem to reproduce traditional phraseology.[55] Paul's own interest in the story of Abraham is focused at other points. The understanding of the atonement as reward for the Akedah might even seem to run contrary to Paul's point of view, indeed to an extent that would exclude his incorporating fragments of a tradition that expressed this idea. Yet, on closer examination, the theory of dependence is confirmed rather than disproved. Stressing that the atonement excludes the kauchēsis (of the Jews), Paul goes on to argue that not even Abraham had anything to boast of.[56] His reward was given kata charin and not kata opheilēma. (It is not denied that he was rewarded!)[57] Concentrating upon interpretation of Genesis 15:6, Paul avoids any direct reference to Genesis 22, even where we might have expected one.[58] As it would not have been difficult to argue that the trial was a test of Abraham's faith, Paul may have avoided doing so for the sake of simplicity.

Paul's use of the ancient Jewish-Christian tradition implies a critical interpretation, sharply formulated in the statement, "There is no distinction."[59] Yet Paul did not contradict the old tradition but incorporated it in a new context. He recognized "Jew first" to be a principle of divine economy and reckoned both "the oracles of God" and "the fathers" among the privileges granted to the Israelites.[60] Even when the order was reversed, Gentiles believing the gospel and Jews rejecting it, Paul insisted that the Israelites were "beloved for the sake of the fathers."[61] At the end of his letter to the Romans Paul can summarize in words that fully conform to the Jewish-Christian interpretation we have been tracing, "Christ became a servant to the circumcised to show God's truthfulness, in order to confirm the promises given to the fathers, and in

order that the Gentiles might glorify God for his mercy," etc.[62]
Both directly and indirectly evidence from Paul's letters supports the conjecture that he was familiar with Jewish-Christian
interpretation of the promises given to the fathers, especially
in Genesis 22:16-18.

                                    III

     It has been surmised, and may today be generally accepted,
that to the earliest churches in Judea the ministry, death and
resurrection of Jesus were believed to bring redemption to
Israel, according to the Scriptures. The effect upon the Gentile nations was considered a further consequence, an object
of eschatological hope rather than of missionary efforts.[63]
In this respect my tentative results simply add support to the
scant evidence that this really was the case. If true, however, they would increase our knowledge at another point;
there existed a specifically Jewish-Christian "doctrine of the
atonement," more explicit than has often been assumed on the
basis of Acts. The death of Jesus upon the cross was interpreted as fulfilling what God had promised Abraham by oath:
As Abraham had not withheld his son, so God did not spare his
own Son, but gave him up for Isaac's descendants. As the sacrifice, provided by God, he expiated their former sins. Vicar-
iously he was made a curse to redeem them from the curse caused
by their transgressions of the Law, so that even the Gentile
nations might be blessed in the offspring of Abraham, the crucified Messiah Jesus. That God in his great mercy rewarded
Abraham by acting as the patriarch did at the Akedah would
thus seem to be part of fairly coherent early Jewish Christian
theology in which the crucifixion of Jesus was interpreted in
the light of Genesis 22.

     The fragments surmised to be contained in Paul's letters

to the Romans and the Galatians cannot belong to the very beginnings of Christian doctrine. The interpretation of Genesis 22 presupposes that Jesus was not only identified as the Messiah but also predicated Son of God, in accordance with 2 Samuel 7:14 and Psalm 2:7. By way of analogy not only "offspring of David" but also "offspring" of Abraham was taken to refer to Jesus as the Messiah. Yet, the interpretation must be early, because it would seem to have been germinal to the phrase "God gave his Son,"[64] and possibly to the designations of Jesus as "the only Son" and "the lamb of God."[65]

The use of Genesis 22, attested by the texts we have considered, presupposes some familiarity with aggadic traditions as well as with the biblical text.[66] But it is not possible to assume that current ideas about the vicarious suffering of Isaac were simply taken over and applied to the passion of Jesus.[67] Like the biblical story, the New Testament allusions emphasize the conduct of Abraham and the promise of God. If the motifs had been directly transferred from Isaac to Christ, one would have expected more emphasis upon the voluntary submission of the former, as in the Aggadah. In many respects it would seem better to regard the early Christian interpretation of Genesis 22 as an independent parallel rather than as derived from Jewish Akedah traditions. What the earliest Jewish Christian traditions presuppose is not so much any special features of the Aggadah as the general spiritual climate of Midrash. It cannot be characterized better than in the words of Judah Goldin: "That conviction lies at the heart of Midrash all the time: The Scriptures are not only a record of the past but a prophecy, a foreshadowing and foretelling, of what will come to pass. And if this is the case, text and personal experience are not two autonomous domains. On the contrary, they are reciprocally enlightening: even as the immediate event helps make the age-old text intelligible, so in turn the text reveals the fundamental significance of the recent event or experience."[68] Without alteration this statement might also be applied to early Christian use of Scriptures.

Early Christian use of Scriptures was not differentiated from contemporary Jewish Midrash by some new hermeneutic. The methods of interpretation remained much the same, with variations in various branches both of the primitive church and of Judaism. What caused a basic difference was new events and new experiences. For Judaism, the story of the binding of Isaac provided help in understanding that the God of the fathers allowed the sufferings and death of faithful Jews in the days of Antiochus Epiphanes and later. The same story helped followers of Jesus to overcome the scandal of the cross and to understand what had happened as an act of God's love and a manifestation of his righteousness. For centuries the interpretation of Genesis 22 was a part of the controversy between Christians and Jews, and even the common use of scientific methods has not quite brought the controversy to an end. It is interesting, and may be important, to realize that the earliest Christian interpretation antedates the controversy. Not any competition, but the close correspondence between the Akedah and the atonement was stressed, quite possibly to the extent that the redemption by Christ was seen as an adequate reward for the binding of Isaac.

The essays collected in this volume are only that:
"essays," critical and constructive attempts to come to terms
with some of the major issues which confront the student of the
New Testament and Christian origins. My further work has led
to elaboration rather than to any major revision of the ideas
set forth. I may, eventually, be able to deal with the issues
in a more comprehensive and systematic way; at the present
moment I would just like to add some comments in response to
critics who have objected to the theses set forth in this volume, especially in the opening essay.

It would seem that few, if any, scholars still doubt that
Jesus was indeed crucified as an alleged king of the Jews.
Rudolf Bultmann has himself been willing to change his opinion
at this point. In a private letter (Marburg, Nov. 26, 1964)
he wrote: "I regard it as a special merit that you have emphasized the way in which the historical fact of the execution of
Jesus as 'King of the Jews' led to a christological reinterpretation of the messianic texts and concepts and how the 'fulfilment' of the prophecy is at the same time always a new interpretation. It is a happy coincidence that Dinkler's contribution to the Festschrift contains a confirmation of what you
have stated."[1]

In his major work on The Titles of Jesus in Christology
Ferdinand Hahn writes: "There is not the slightest reason to
doubt the historicity of the inscription on the cross."[2] He
quite correctly stresses that in Paul and other writers the
title "Christ" is closely linked to the passion tradition.
Nevertheless, Hahn thinks that this usage belongs to a somewhat later stage of development; in ancient Palestinian tradi-

tion the title Messiah was first used with reference to the parousia of Jesus. This conclusion is based upon historical reconstruction more than upon clear textual evidence. As Martin Hengel has pointed out, Hahn has failed to see that the fact of the crucifixion immediately confronted the missionary church with the christological problem of the crucified Messiah.[3] One may add that the expectation of Jesus' parousia is a hope for his public vindication.

In a paper entitled "Jesus the Christ" W. C. van Unnik has set forth a view which contrasts sharply with Hahn's reconstruction. He thinks that for the early Christians the essential element in the messiahship of Jesus was "not the outward activity of a king but the person possessed by the Spirit."[4] The main evidence for this is drawn from Luke-Acts where Jesus is represented as the Christ of God who was anointed with the Holy Spirit. As Luke is writing in a biblical and archaic style, it is hard to know how far he really reproduces ancient traditions. Later evidence, both Jewish-Christian and gnostic, makes it likely that the notion of Jesus as the prophet-king anointed with the Holy Spirit was once more widely held than one might assume on the basis of the New Testament writings. But even so, the Lucan representation is only one among several interpretations of the messiahship of Jesus and cannot possibly be the starting point for all later developments. It does not explain the Pauline use of Christos. The Gospels of Matthew and John and the Epistle to the Hebrews demonstrate that even the integration of prophetic (Mosaic) and royal (messianic) features in the portrait of Jesus the Christ could be achieved along other lines.

In his booklet What Do We Know About Jesus? and elsewhere Otto Betz stresses the fundamental importance of the crucifixion of Jesus as "King of the Jews." But he finds it

very strange that I proposed a solution which would make Caiaphas and Pilate the indirect originators of christology.[5] Betz
thinks that one has to move backward and conclude that Jesus
knew himself to be the Messiah and that he for the first time
publicly confessed this at the trial. But would it really be
so strange if the title "Messiah" should have been attributed
to Jesus by people who misunderstood him, accused him, and
mocked him but was later taken up by those who proclaimed and
praised the crucified Messiah whom God had raised from the dead?
Would not this turning of the tables harmonize very well with a
biblical theme which is pregnantly stated in the saying about
the rejected stone?

Betz has seen that the trial scene in Mark 14:53-64 alludes to the Nathan oracle in 2 Samuel 7. But as Donald H.
Juel has shown in a recent Yale dissertation, the account of
the trial, like the whole passion narrative in Mark, is composed from the perspective of Christian faith in such a way
that enemies and false witnesses are made to attest the veiled
messiahship of the crucified Jesus.[6] The trial scene is a
literary composition from which one cannot draw any historical
inferences, except that Jesus does not seem to have denied his
alleged messiahship.

What is said about the high priest would apply to the
Messiah also: "Nobody arrogates the honour to himself: he is
called by God" (Heb. 5:4 NEB). If this is correct, and it
might be elaborated in some detail, both adherents and opponents may have considered Jesus a potential Messiah even though
he did not claim to be so. In a stimulating article J. C.
O'Neill has gone further and argued that "The Silence of Jesus"
was part of his messianic role.[7] But if Jesus kept silent, the
evidence is as ambiguous to us as it probably was to his own
contemporaries. The confession that the crucified Jesus was

163

indeed the Anointed One cannot simply be understood as a reaf-
firmation of a claim made by Jesus himself.

Ragnar Leivestad has attacked my position from still another angle.[8] In an article which has only been published in
Norwegian he raises the question: "Was there any alternative
to Messiah?" His answer is a renewal of a theory which was
widely held by nineteenth century critics: Messiah was the
only available title which could express Jesus' unique and
decisive vocation as the last and greatest agent of God. There
was no alternative! If I have understood him correctly, Leivestad thinks that I have gone astray because I have tried to
solve a problem which does not exist.

A counter-critique would have to include a renewed treatment of Jewish expectations. Since Leivestad has not paid any
attention to my essay on "History and Eschatology" I feel free
to abstain from that. It may be sufficient to say that he un-
duly formalizes the concept of Messiah and at the same time
fails to take due account of the variability of Jewish eschatology. I see no proof for his assertion that the Qumran texts
presuppose the use of "the Messiah" as a technical term, and so
on.

It would be futile to discuss what might have happened if
Jesus had not been accused and executed as "King of the Jews."
But the data prove that the unique and decisive role of Jesus
might be expressed in several ways. He could be described in
prophetic categories, as one who was even greater than Moses.
From an early date onward Christians also spoke about him in
terms and phrases which had previously been used about divine
attributes and agents and even about God himself. (The trans-
fer of "God-language" to Jesus is an aspect of early Christology which has been neglected in most recent studies.)

At one essential point I agree with Leivestad. "The Son

of man" was hardly an alternative to "Messiah." Like him and
a number of other scholars I have become increasingly skeptical
against the existence of an apocalyptic Son of man concept in
pre-Christian Judaism. As a consequence, I have had to abandon
the theory that Jesus understood himself as "the hidden Son of
man." The term is enigmatic. Its use by Jesus and in the Gospels may illustrate the possibility that new terms could be
coined to express the unique vocation of Jesus.

It might be objected that many other titles and types of
language are used about Jesus the Messiah; this would seem to
be Leivestad's opinion. But there is at least one branch of
early Christian tradition which does not use the title "Christ"
and yet leaves no doubt about the unique role of Jesus. This
is the tradition of the sayings of Jesus, as represented not
only by the sayings common to Matthew and Luke (the Q source),
but also by sayings incorporated into the Fourth Gospel, and
by the Gospel of Thomas. Yet, it is quite clear that these
sayings were not simply used as a paraenetic supplement to the
kerygma and the gospel story. They were not simply sayings of
the historical Jesus but "words of the living Jesus," as it is
said in the preface to the Gospel of Thomas. As such they are
"the words of eternal life," as it is said in John 6:68. As
has been made clear by several recent studies, already the
tradition common to Matthew and Luke implies a christological
conception, a "christology" in which the title Christos plays
no role.[9]

The relationship between the proclamation of Jesus as the
crucified and risen Christ and the ongoing preaching of the
words of Jesus still calls for further clarification. The four
Gospels, the letters of Paul, and other documents demonstrate
that the two entities could be integrated in several ways.
Their interrelation is a problem within early Christianity

165

which has been obscured by slogans like "the historical Jesus"
and "the kerygmatic Christ." This has been neglected in my
essays on christological origins. But the observation that
the title _Christos_ is used whenever the crucifixion and resurrection of Jesus are proclaimed as the events of salvation,
but not when eternal life is communicated by means of the ongoing tradition of sayings of Jesus, confirms my main thesis.

FOOTNOTES

The Crucified Messiah

1 M. Kähler, The So-Called Historical Jesus and the His-
toric Biblical Christ (tr. C. Braaten; Philadelphia: Fortress,
1964), 47: "For the cardinal virtue of genuine historical
research is modesty." Kähler did not clearly express his
opinion about the possibility of genuine historical research
into the life of Jesus, but he obviously did not want to exclude this possibility.

2 Particularly noteworthy was the article by E. Käsemann,
"The Problem of the Historical Jesus," first published in 1954
and now included in his Essays on New Testament Themes (tr.
W. G. Montague; Naperville: Allenson, 1964), 15-47. Independently of Käsemann, however, several other scholars worked with
the problem. James M. Robinson (A New Quest of the Historical
Jesus SBT 25; Naperville: Allenson, 1959) presents recent
scholarship too one-sidedly as a reaction to Käsemann. My
article, "The Problem of the Historical Jesus," (pp. 48-89 in
this volume) goes back to a paper read in Uppsala in 1952.

3 Cf. "The Problem of the Historical Jesus," pp. 72-74
below.

4 R. Bultmann, Glauben und Verstehen (2nd ed.; Tübingen:
Mohr, 1954), I, 241.

5 To clarify this point I refer to two of my essays, Die
Passionsgeschichte bei Matthäus, (NTS 2, 1955-56, 17-32) and
"Markusevangeliets sikte" (SEA 22-23, 1957-58, 99-112).

6 Cf. R. Bultmann, The History of the Synoptic Tradition
(tr. J. Marsh; New York: Harper, 1963), 280ff.

7 J. Kroll, Gott und Hölle: Der Mythos vom Decensuskampfe
(Berlin: Teubner, 1932), 123f., 529f., etc.

8 Cf. the analysis of biblical narratives, including the
exposition of the denial of Peter in E. Auerbach, Mimesis: The
Representation of Reality in Western Literature (tr. W. Trask;
Princeton: Princeton University Press, 1953), chapters 1 and 2,
esp. 40-49.

9 A. Schweitzer, The Mystery of the Kingdom of God (New
York: Macmillan, 1955). Appeared in German in 1901.

10 A. Schweitzer, The Quest of the Historical Jesus (3rd ed.;
London: Black, 1954), 328-349. (According to Schweitzer, Judas
betrayed the messianic secret!)

11 Schweitzer, Quest, 335. Cf. against this T. W. Manson, "The Life of Jesus, Some Tendencies in present-day Research," The Background of the New Testament and its Eschatology (Cambridge: Cambridge University Press, 1956), 211-221.

12 Bultmann, History, 284; cf. 272-273.

13 Against Bultmann, History, 272. The historicity of the inscription of the charge has been championed recently by T. A. Burkill, "The Trial of Jesus," VC 12 (1958), 1-18; P. Winter, On the Trial of Jesus (Berlin: Walter de Gruyter, 1961), 107-110; W. Meeks, The Prophet-King (Leiden: Brill, 1967), 79, note 1.

14 Cf. P. Borgen, "John and the Synoptics in the Passion Narrative," NTS 5 (1958), 246-259.

15 Cf. John 18:36f., 19:21f.; Matt. 27:17, 22 (Mark 15:9, 12), as well as the absence of Lukan parallels to Mark 15:9, 12, 18.

16 The difficulties encountered if one seeks to understand the application of the title "Messiah" to Jesus purely from the study of the history of ideas are quite evident in the rather inadequate treatment "Jesus the Messiah" in O. Cullmann's The Christology of the New Testament (tr. S. Guthrie and C. Hall; Philadelphia: Westminster, 1959), 111-137. The same difficulties are present in F. Hahn, The Titles of Jesus in Christology, their History in Early Christianity (tr. H. Knight and G. Ogg; London: Lutterworth Press, 1969), 136-239; and R. Fuller, The Foundations of New Testament Christology (New York: Scribner's, 1965).

17 It would, of course, be otherwise if the supposition were true that the Caesarea-Philippi pericope and the transfiguration story were transposed Easter stories. But there is no basis for this assumption apart from the supposition that the disciples' faith in the Messiah was grounded in their Easter visions.

18 This has been correctly seen by S. L. Edgar, "New Testament and Rabbinic Messianic Interpretation," NTS 5 (1958), 47-54.

19 Cf. J. A. T. Robinson, "Elijah, John and Jesus," NTS 4 (1958), 263-281.

20 John 1:19ff.; 7:26f., 40ff.; 12:34. Cf. Bent Noack, "Johannes-evangeliets messiasbillede og dets kristologi," DTT 19 (1956), 129-155; M. de Jonge, NTS 19 (1972-73), 246-270.

21 Cf. esp. A. Vögtle, Messiasbekenntnis und Petrusverheissung," BZ n.F. 1 (1957), 252-272; 2 (1958), 85-103.

22 G. Bornkamm, Jesus of Nazareth (tr. Irene McLuskey et al; New York: Harper and Row, 1960), 172.

23 On the methodological difficulties, cf. J. M. Robinson, A New Quest, 100ff.

24 Cf. on this H. E. Tödt, The Son of Man in the Synoptic Tradition (tr. D. Barton; Philadelphia: Westminster, 1965); and E. Schweizer, "Der Menschensohn," and "The Son of Man again" in Neotestamentica (Zurich: Zwingli-Verlag, 1963), 56-84 and 85-92.

25 Mark 10:38, Luke 12:50. The word "be baptized" (or "be immersed") seems to be used here not in the Christian sacramental sense, but in the more general Jewish ritual sense.

26 Thus E. Sjöberg, Der verborgene Menschensohn in den Evangelien (Lund: Gleerup, 1955), 241.

27 "The Problem of the Historical Jesus," 45.

28 Cf. on this Ottar Dahl, Om årsaksproblemer i historisk forskning (Oslo: University Press, 1956), with an English summary: Problems of causation in historical research.

29 Bornkamm, Jesus, 172.

30 The greatest difficulty in Mark 14:55-64 is that Jesus' messianic claim is the occasion for his condemnation on the grounds of blasphemy. This is most easily explained as the viewpoint of the narrator, who knew well that the Christian confession of Jesus' messiahship was a scandal and blasphemy to Jews. It is quite probable that the High Priest was concerned to find some basis for a charge before Pilate. The individual problems cannot be dealt with here. I do believe that in 14:62 the reading "You say that I am" is worthy of consideration. I regard Stauffer's interpretation of this verse as fantastic (Jesus and His Story, tr. R. and C. Winston, New York: Knopf, 1960), 124, 184.

31 E. Fuchs, "The Quest of the Historical Jesus," Studies of the Historical Jesus (tr. A. Scobie; Naperville: Allenson, 1964), 11-31.

32 I have been unable to deal here with Christ's resurrection. But in my way of approaching historical questions I feel a certain kinship with the work of Hans von Campenhausen, "The Events of Easter and the Empty Tomb," in Tradition and Life in the Church (tr. A. V. Littledale, Philadelphia: Fortress, 1968), 42-89.

The Messiahship of Jesus in Paul

1 As a rule, this question is treated briefly in expositions
of Pauline theology and in commentaries, e.g. von Dobschütz on
1 Thess. 1:1 (Die Thessalonicher-Briefe   Meyer; Göttingen:
Vandenhoeck und Ruprecht, 1909   ) and Lietzmann on Rom. 1:1
(An die Römer   HNT, 8; Tübingen: Mohr, 1928   ). The most
detailed treatments in recent years are L. Cerfaux, Christ in
the Theology of St. Paul (tr. G. Webb and A. Walker ; New York:
Herder & Herder, 1959), 480-505, and W. Kramer, Christ, Lord,
Son of God (tr. Brian Hardy; Naperville: Allenson, 1966).

2 Christos Iēsous is quite well-attested in manuscripts
(Gal. 5:24, 6:12; Eph. 3:1, 11; Col. 2:6); Iēsous Christos in
comparison occurs infrequently (Gal. 5:24; Col. 2:6).

3 Only rarely "Jesus" (1 Thess. 4:14); "Jesus Christ" or
"Christ Jesus" (Rom. 8:34; 2 Cor. 13:5; Gal. 3:1); "the Lord
Jesus" (1 Cor. 11:23; 2 Thess. 2:8 v.l.; cf. 1 Thess. 3:11).
2 Thess. 2:16 is unique.

4 In the introductory greetings, apo . . . kyriou Iēsou
Christou is a standard formula; cf. also Eph. 6:23, (Phil.
3:20), 1 Thess. 1:1; 2 Thess. 1:1, 12. The genitive tou
kyriou is usually found with charis; tou kyriou hēmōn Iēsou
Christou also occurs with onoma, patēr, parousia, hēmera, etc.
Finally, dia Iēsou Christou tou kyriou hēmōn and en Christō
Iēsou tō kyriō hēmōn are frequently used formulas.

5 en Iēsou Christō only in Gal. 3:14 (cod Ν & B); dia
Christou Iēsou in Rom. 2:16 (cod Ν & B). en tō Iēsou in
Eph. 4:21 is striking.

6 In 1 Cor. 11:3 and Col. 1:7 the nouns are only formally
anarthrous.

7 Rom. 14:8; 2 Cor. 11:2; Eph. 2:5, 5:24, 6:5; Col. 3:1.
Without the article only in Gal. 2:19: Christō synestaurōmai.

8 Cf. Blass-Debrunner, A Greek Grammar of the New Testament
(tr. and ed. R. Funk; Chicago: University of Chicago Press,
1961), par 260, 1. The articular form is found regularly in
comparisons, kathōs kai ho Christos (Rom. 15:3, 7; Eph. 5:2,
23, 25, 29; cf. 1 Cor. 12:12). Ephesians deviates from the
pattern of the other epistles mainly because of the frequency
of formulas like en tō Christō (1:10, 12, 20, cf. 3:11).

9 Cf. on this Cerfaux, op. cit., 481-484; the overly-
ingenious work of W. Schmauch, In Christus (Gütersloh: Bertels-

mann, 1935); and W. Kramer, Christ, Lord, Son of God, 19-64.

10 Thus von Dobschütz, Die Thessalonicher-Briefe, 61. Similarly, but more cautiously, R. Bultmann, Theology of the New Testament (tr. K. Grobel; New York: Scribner's, 1951), I, 80. Cf. also notes 6 and 7 above.

11 1 Cor. 10:4, 15:22; 2 Cor. 5:10, 11:2f.; Eph. 1:10, 12, 20, 5:14; Phil. 1:15, 17, 3:7. But in no case in Paul can Christos be translated with "Messiah."

12 Cf. 1 Cor. 1:23; Rom. 15:7; Gal. 3:16. In 1 Cor. 1:23 we certainly do not find any antithesis to a Messiah who is not crucified.

13 On the other hand, in 1 and 2 Peter, James, Jude, and Hebrews, as in Paul, it is never necessary to understand the term as a title.

14 This is true above all in Acts in the expression "the name of Jesus Christ" (2:38, 3:6, 4:10), which perhaps sheds light on the origin of the usage.

15 Cf. also 2 John 9; Matt. 1:17, 11:2; Acts 2:31, 8:5, 26:23; Rev. 20:4, 10; etc. Here the appellatival significance is still clear to some degree, whereas it is not in the Apostolic Fathers (1 Clement, 2 Clement, Ignatius, Polycarp).

16 Christos is to be understood as a title in Matt. 1:18 (cod B only) and in Acts 3:20 and 5:42, but as a proper name in Acts 24:24; the textual history is ambiguous. Later the sequence Christos Iēsous is found in Ignatius (Magn. 8:2, 10:3 v.l.; Rom. 6:1 v.l.; etc.) and in Polycarp (Phil. 8:1), as well as in the Old Roman Symbol. On the other hand it occurs in 1 Clement only in the Pauline expression en Christō Iēsou (32:3, 38:1); the expression occurs frequently in Ignatius, even alongside the non-Pauline en Iēsou Christō (Ign. Eph. 8:2, 10:3, etc.).

17 Cf. the secondary insertion of the article in 1 Cor. 3:11 and Acts 5:42, 9:34. Iēsous ho Christos occurs also in 1 Clem. 42:1 and Ign. Eph. 18:2. It is strange that later Christ's priestly dignity in particular has been bound up with the name Christ; cf. e.g. Tert. Adv. Marc. III, 7; Cyr. Kat. X, 4, 11, 14 (already in Just. Dial. 86:3, 141:3 ?). The concept of the threefold office is likewise combined with the name Christ (Eus. H. E. I, 3; Dem. Ev. IV, 15, VIII, preface; similarly Calvin Inst. II, 15, and many after him).

18 Bousset's perception here must not be obscured by all the criticism of his Kyrios Christos (tr. J. Steely; Nashville: Abingdon, 1971). Yet we must also reckon with the possibility that already in Judaism "Messiah" was on the way to becoming a proper name (cf. the malkā mešihā of the Targums and Christos kyrios in Lam. 4:20 and Ps. Sol. 17:32--unless the text has

undergone Christian alteration).

19 „W. Wrede, Paul (tr. E. Lummis; London: P. Green, 1907).
M. Brückner, Die Entstehung der paulinischen Christologie
(Strassburg: J. H. E. Heitz, 1903).

20 Cf. Bultmann, Theology I, 123ff.

21 This is clearly the case, e.g., in Rom. 1:3-4; Gal. 4:4;
Col. 1:13; 1 Thess. 1:10. In the background stands the messi-
anic-christological interpretation of Psalm 2.

22 Cf. Acts 2:34, Rom. 8:34, 1 Cor. 15:25, Eph. 1:20, Col.
3:1.

23 Cf. Rom. 4:25; 10:16 and 15:21; 9:33; 11:26; 15:3, 8-11;
Eph. 2:13-17; 4:8; further, Gal. 3 and Rom. 4. By christological interpretation of the Old Testament Paul also arrives at
a conception of the presence of Christ in OT history (1 Cor.
10:1ff.). On Gal. 3, cf. below pp. 142, 153f. with notes.

24 Cf. e.g. 1 Thess. 4:14-17, 5:1ff.; 2 Thess. 1:7-10, 2:8;
Rom. 11:26; 2 Cor. 5:10.

25 Gal. 4:4; cf. Eph. 1:10.

26 Col. 1:18; cf. 1 Cor. 15:20ff.

27 1 Cor. 15:45-49, cf. 15:22; Rom. 5:12ff., cf. Eph. 2:15
and 5:31. To what extent other, perhaps gnostic conceptions
are involved does not need to be discussed here.

28 Rom. 1:4, Phil. 2:9-11, Eph. 1:19-23, Col. 3:1f., etc.

29 Cf. esp. Rom. 4; 1 Cor. 10:1ff.; Gal. 3:29, 6:16.

30 At this point Albert Schweitzer's basic conception has
essentially advanced interpretation of Paul in spite of all
one-sidedness and poor exegesis. Concerning the doctrine of
justification, cf. H. D. Wendland, Die Mitte der paulinischen
Botschaft (Göttingen: Vandenhoeck und Ruprecht, 1935).

31 Gal. 4:4, 3:13; Rom. 7:4, cf. Gal. 2:19.

32 On the problem, cf. H. Bietenhard, Das tausendjährige
Reich (Bern: F. Graf-Lehmann, 1944).

The Problem of the Historical Jesus

1 This essay originally appeared in a collection of lectures entitled <u>Rett laere og kjetterske meninger</u> (Oslo, 1953). The revised German draft still gives evidence of the fact that the author has attempted to write in an intelligible way also for nontheologians, which accounts for a certain breadth and scope in presentation.

2 W. Montgomery tr., (New York: The Macmillan Company, 1948), p. 3. Used by permission of The Macmillan Company and A. & C. Black, Ltd.

3 <u>Ibid</u>., p. 4.

4 <u>Die Gleichnisreden Jesu</u>, I (Tübingen: J. C. B. Mohr, 1910), 144.

5 <u>The Messianic Secret</u> (tr. J. C. G. Green, Greenwood, S.C.: Attic Press), p. 6.

6 Berlin: Georg Reimer, 1905, p. 114.

7 Göttingen: Vandenhoeck und Ruprecht, 1892, p. v. ET, <u>Jesus' Proclamation of the Kingdom of God</u> (Philadelphia: Fortress, 1971).

8 Schweitzer, <u>op</u>. <u>cit</u>., p. 396.

9 <u>Ibid</u>., p. 397.

10 Gösta Lindeskog has written the history of this research in <u>Die Jesusfrage im neuzeitlichen Judentum</u> (Uppsala, 1938). Cf. also <u>Judaica</u>, VI (1950), 190-229, 241-68.

11 Wellhausen, <u>op</u>. <u>cit</u>., p. 113.

12 <u>Ibid</u>., p. 115.

13 Schweitzer, <u>op</u>. <u>cit</u>., p. 401.

14 Cf. Käsemann, <u>Essays on New Testament Themes</u>, pp. 15ff.

15 Stauffer, "Der Stand der neutestamentlichen Forschung," <u>Theologie und Liturgie</u>, ed. L. Henning (1952), pp. 35-105. Cf. <u>Jesus and His Story</u>.

16 Cf. my essay, "Die Passionsgeschichte bei Matthäus, <u>NTS</u> 2 (1955-56), 17-32.

17 Joachim Jeremias, The Parables of Jesus, tr. S. H. Hooke (New York: Charles Scribners Sons, 1955), pp. 20-28.

18 Julius Schniewind's remarks in "Zur Synoptikerexegese," Theologische Rundschau, II (1930), 129-89, are still of value, and particularly his discussion of "longitudinal" and "cross-section exegesis." On the questions of method, cf. also C. H. Dodd, History and the Gospel (London: James Nisbet & Company, 1938).

19 Käsemann, Essays, p. 37.

20 Stauffer, op. cit., p. 93.

21 Wellhausen, op. cit., p. 115.

22 Here, the starting point of C. F. W. Smith, The Jesus of the Parables (Philadelphia: The Westminster Press, 1948), p. 17, is correct: "Jesus used parables and Jesus was put to death. The two factors are related and it is necessary to understand the connection." On the exposition of the parables cf. also my essay, "The Parables of Growth," Studia Theologica, 5 (1951), 132-66.

23 Hans Freiherr von Campenhausen, Tradition and Life, pp. 42-89.

24 Cf. Bultmann, Faith and Understanding (ed. and tr. R. W. Funk and L. P. Smith, New York: Harper and Row, 1969), I, 206.

25 Bultmann, Theology, I, 165f.

26 On this cf. my review article, pp. 90-128 in this volume, esp. pp. 96f., 113, 127.

27 Bultmann, Theology, I, 8.

28 Cf., e.g., Bultmann, Faith and Understanding, I, 237f.

29 Cf. especially Albert Schweitzer, The Mysticism of Paul the Apostle (New York: Macmillan, 1955), pp. 113-115; 389-396. In addition, cf. also Rudolf Bultmann, "Jesus and Paul," Existence and Faith, tr. Schubert M. Ogden (New York: Meridian Books, 1960), pp. 183-201.

30 This is the Church, ed. Anders Nygren et al., tr. Carl C. Rasmussen (Philadelphia: Muhlenberg Press, 1952), p. 22.

31 Anton Fridrichsen, et al., The Root of the Vine (London: Dacre Press, 1953), p. 60.

32 Cf. Jeremias, op. cit., pp. 25-28.

33 On this question cf. W. Michaelis, "Notwendigkeit und Grenze der Erörterung von Echtheitsfragen innerhalb des Neuen Testaments," Theologische Literatur-Zeitung (1952), pp. 97-402.

FOOTNOTES

Rudolf Bultmann's Theology of the New Testament

1 R. Bultmann, Theology of the New Testament (tr. K. Grobel; New York: Scribner's, 1951 and 1955; original German publication in 1948-1953).

2 F. Büchsel, Theologie des Neuen Testaments (Gütersloh: Bertelsmann, 1935); E. Stauffer, New Testament Theology (tr. J. Marsh; London: SCM Press, 1955); F. Grant, An Introduction to the New Testament Thought (Nashville: Abingdon, 1950); M. Goguel, The Birth of Christianity (tr. H. C. Snape; New York: Macmillan, 1954; original French publication in 1946) and The Primitive Church (tr. H. C. Snape; New York: Macmillan, 1964; original publication in 1948). The impressive scope of Bultmann's Theology stands out even in light of works published after his.

3 G. Kittel and G. Friedrich, eds., Theological Dictionary of the New Testament (tr. G. Bromiley; Grand Rapids: Eerdmans, 1964-1974.

4 In this regard, comparison with Gerhard von Rad's Old Testament Theology (tr. D. Stalker; New York: Harper and Row, 1965), is illuminating.

5 H. Weinel, Biblische Theologie des Neuen Testaments (4th ed.; Tübingen: Mohr, 1928).

6 One of the real differences between Barth and Bultmann has been from the outset their theological point of departure; for Barth, it is the situation of the preacher, for Bultmann, the situation of the hearer of the word.

7 Thus O. Cullmann, Christ and Time (tr. F. V. Filson; Philadelphia: Westminster, 1950), 26.

8 Cf. Karl Barth, "Rudolf Bultmann--An Attempt to Understand Him," Kerygma and Myth (ed. H. W. Bartsch; tr. R. H. Fuller; London: S.P.C.K., 1962), II, 83-132. Barth comes to the conclusion that Bultmann is primarily to be understood as standing in a Lutheran tradition. I find it remarkable that Bultmann does in fact implicitly accept this as a basis for discussion. This I infer from what I take to be his reply, the counter-criticism of Barth in "Adam and Christ according to Romans 5," Current Issues in New Testament Interpretation (ed. W. Klassen and G. F. Snyder; New York: Harper, 1962), 143-165.

9 Cf. Gerhard Gloege, Mythologie und Luthertum (Berlin: Lutherisches Verlagshaus, 1952), p. 43.

10 For Bultmann's distinction between "existential" and "existentiell," cf. Jesus Christ and Mythology (New York: Scribner's, 1958), 66 as explicated on p. 74.

11 R. Bultmann, Essays Philosophical and Theological (tr. J. C. G. Greig; London: SCM Press, 1955), 234ff.

12 Cf. also Bultmann's Gifford Lectures, History and Eschatology (Edinburgh: Edinburgh University Press, 1957).

13 It is unfortunate that the discussion of Bultmann's theology has often dealt more with his essay "New Testament and Mythology" (Kerygma and Myth, I, 1-44   ) than with his major works.

14 The booklet published by Wrede in 1897 has finally been translated. Cf. "The Task and Methods of 'New Testament Theology'" in Robert Morgan, The Nature of New Testament Theology (SBT II 25; London: SCM, 1973), pp. 68-116.

15 In his book Primitive Christianity in its Contemporary Setting (tr. R. H. Fuller; New York: World Publishing Company, 1956), Bultmann deals with the preaching of Jesus in the section on Judaism. Bultmann has subsequently defended his position in "The Primitive Christian Kerygma and the Historical Jesus" which is included in The Historical Jesus and the Kerygmatic Christ (tr. and ed. C. E. Braaten and R. A. Harrisville, New York: Abingdon, 1964), pp. 15-42.

16 Cf. M. Dibelius, Gospel Criticism and Christology (London: Ivor Nicholson and Watson, 1935).

17 Jesus and the Word (tr. L. P. Smith and E. H. Lantero, New York: Scribner's, 1934; German edition, 1925).

18 It is typical that Ernst Percy in his Die Botschaft Jesu (Lund: Gleerup, 1953) organized much of his work as a discussion with Bultmann.

19 Cf. my remarks on the problem of method in "The Problem of the Historical Jesus," pp. 63-74 in this volume.

20 Cf. H. J. Schoeps, Theologie und Geschichte der Judenchristentums (Tübingen: Mohr, 1949), and Bultmann's critical review in Gnomon 26 (1954), 187-189.

21 Cf. my essay "The Messiahship of Jesus in Paul," in this volume, pp. 37-47.

22 Cf. C. H. Dodd, According to the Scriptures (London: Nisbet, 1953); B. Lindars, New Testament Apologetic (Philadelphia: Westminster, 1961).

23 W. Bousset, Kyrios Christos (tr. J. Steely; Nashville: Abingdon, 1970; first German edition in 1913).

24   It is regrettable that the essay of Lyder Brun ("Urmenig-hetens Kristustro," Norsk teologi til reformasjonsjubilaeet, NovTSup 18, 1917 , 80-128), owing to language and circumstances of time, has been overlooked in the German debate regarding Bousset's views.

25   Primitive Christianity, 175. Cf. H. Gunkel, Zum religions-geschichtlichen Verstandnis des Neuen Testaments (Göttingen: Vandenhoeck und Ruprecht, 1903).

26   Cf. Hans Jonas, The Gnostic Religion (Boston: Beacon Press, 1958).

27   Cf. also his preface to the third German edition.

28   Bultmann writes that when the expectation of the early church is one day fulfilled, this fulfillment will never be-come a past, a source of confidence on which one gratefully looks back, as Israel looked back on the crossing of the Red Sea. It will be God's last deed by which he puts an end to history (I, 36). The Rabbis, in contrast, discuss only whether in the days of the Messiah men will mention in prayer only the messianic redemption or will still remember the exodus from Egypt (Mishnah Berakoth 1:5; cf. bBerakoth 12b-13a). I suspect that early Palestinian Christians thought as the Rabbis rather than as Bultmann.

29   Bultmann's view does find support in the works of H. Conzelmann The Theology of St. Luke (tr. G. Buswell; New York: Harper and Row, 1961) and E. Haenchen The Acts of the Apostles (tr. B. Noble et al.; Philadelphia: Westminster, 1971), but these authors have not spoken the last word.

30   I, 238f. Cf. W. Mundle, Der Glaubensbegriff des Paulus (Leipzig: M. Heinsius, 1932), 99ff.

31   Cf. Kerygma and Myth, I, 10f.

32   Cf. Jesus Christ and Mythology, 70f.

Eschatology and History in Light of the Qumran Texts

1 This essay is a revised form of a guest lecture given at the universities of Utrecht and Heidelberg.

2 The Epistle to the Romans (tr. E. C. Hoskins; London: Oxford University Press, 1933; 2nd German edition in 1922), 314.

3 History and Eschatology (New York: Harper & Brothers, 1957).

4 Cf. my review of Bultmann's Theology of the New Testament in this volume, pp. 90-128.

5 Jesus and the Word (tr. L. Pettibone Smith; New York: Scribner's, 1934), 35.

6 History and Eschatology, 23.

7 Ibid., 151 and 154. Cf. his Theology of the New Testament (tr. K. Grobel; New York: Scribner's, 1959), I, 306; "New Testament and Mythology," Kerygma and Myth (ed. H. W. Bartsch; tr. R. Fuller; New York: Harper, 1954), I, 29.

8 Paul and his Interpreters (tr. W. Montgomery; London: A. and C. Black, 1912), 228.

9 The Mysticism of Paul the Apostle (tr. W. Montgomery; New York: Macmillan, 1955), p. 54.

10 Cf. e.g. A. Dillmann, Liber Henoch (Leipzig, 1851) and his Das Buch Henoch (Leipzig: Vogel, 1853); A. Hilgenfeld, Die jüdische Apokalyptik (Jena: F. Mauke, 1857).

11 W. Baldensperger, Das Selbstbewusstsein Jesu im Lichte der messianischen Hoffnungen seiner Zeit (Strassburg: Heitz, 1888); S. Mowinckel, He that Cometh (tr. G. W. Anderson; New York: Abingdon, 1956); Bousset-Gressmann, Die Religion des Judentums (Berlin: Reuter und Reichard, 1926[3]).

12 A. Dupont-Sommer, The Dead Sea Scrolls: a Preliminary Survey (tr. E. M. Rowley; Oxford: Blackwell, 1952) and The Essene Writings from Qumran (tr. G. Vermes; New York: Meridian Books, 1962); H. Kosmala, Hebräer -- Essener -- Christen (Leiden: Brill, 1959); G. Friedrich, "Beobachtungen zur messianischen Hohepriestererwartung in den Synoptikern," ZThK 53 (1956), 265-311.

13 G. Jeremias, _Der Lehrer der Gerechtigkeit_ (Studien zur Umwelt des NT, 2; Göttingen: Vandenhoeck und Ruprecht, 1963), 321.

14 _The Scrolls and the New Testament_ (New York: Harper, 1957), 1-17.

15 Cf. the preface to the 3rd German edition of his _Theologie_.

16 IQS 9:10f. (Unless otherwise noted, all English translations of Qumran material are taken from Dupont-Sommer's _The Essene Writings from Qumran_, cited above.)

17 CD vi, 10f.; xii, 23f.; xx, 1. Cf. 4QPB 3f.

18 L. Ginzberg, _Eine unbekannte jüdische sekte_ (New York: 1922), pp. 303ff.

19 More precisely, Ex. 20:21b, according to a text that agrees with the Samaritan Pentateuch. Cf. J. T. Milik, _Ten Years of Discoveries in the Wilderness of Judea_ (SBT 26; tr. J. Strugnell; Naperville: Allenson, 1959), 124 note 1 (following Skehan); and further, 4Qbibpar 158, fragment 6.

20 4QT. R. Meyer ("'Eliah' und 'Ahab'," _Abraham Unser Vater: Festschrift für O. Michel_ Leiden: Brill, 1963 , 356-368) would relate all three testimonies to the "teacher of righteousness." Given the general structure of the sect and its teachings, however, it is most improbable that the teacher was viewed as the bearer of the threefold office. Cf. G. Jeremias, _op. cit._, and A. S. van der Woude, _Die messianischen Vorstellungen der Gemeinde von Qumran_ (Assen: Van Gorcum, 1957).

21 The three figures are basically contemporaneous even if one assumes that the high priest or Elijah will already be present at the appearance of the Messiah. Cf. e.g. 4QF 1, 11 and Justin _Dial_ 8. In a similar way the Messiah, Elijah and the Prophet are each mentioned in John 1:20f., perhaps as bearers of the three offices. The conception of Elijah as the eschatological high priest is pre-Christian, attested for the time of John Hyrcanus by Targum Pseudo-Jon on Deut. 32:11. Cf. R. Meyer, "'Eliah' und 'Ahab'," 356ff., and S. Schulz, "Die Bedeutung der neuen Targumforschung," _Abraham Unser Vater_, 434f. (following Geiger).

22 Josephus, _Antig._ 13, 299; _Bell_. 1, 68. Cf. e.g. R. Meyer, _Der Prophet aus Galiläa_ (Leipzig, 1940), 60ff.; _TDNT_ VI, 825f.

23 In a still unpublished text from Cave 4 the true prophet is to be recognized by the anointed priest. Cf. Milik, _op. cit._, 126. On the prophet, cf. among others H. M. Teeple, _The Mosaic Eschatological Prophet_ (JBL Monograph Series 10; Philadelphia:

SBL, 1957).

24 IQSb 5:20-29; IQM 11:6f.; 4QPB; 4QT; 4QpIs[a]; CD vii, 19f.
Cf. on this van der Woude, op. cit., passim, though he has not
systematically investigated the question of scriptural basis
for Qumran doctrine concerning the Messiah.

25 Cf. esp. 4QFl; in addition, 4QPB 2-4. From pre-Christian
Judaism the following may be mentioned: Sir. 45:25; Ps. Sol.
17:4. From the NT: Heb. 1:5, 3:2, 6; Rom. 1:3f.; Luke 1:32f.,
22:28-30; Acts 2:30, 13:22, 32ff.; Rev. 22:16; perhaps also
Matt. 16:16-18; 22:41-44; Mark 14:57-62; John 8:35. Cf. A. van
Iersel, "Der Sohn" in den synoptischen Jesusworten (Leiden:
Brill, 1961); E. Lövestam, Son and Savior (Lund: Gleerup,
1961); S. Aalen, "'Reign' and 'House'," NTS 8 (1962), 215-240,
esp. 233-240. For the OT, G. von Rad, Old Testament Theology
(tr. D. M. G. Stalker; New York: Harper and Row, 1962, 1965),
I, 40f. and 318ff.; II, 45f. The question of age and original
wording of the oracle of Nathan may remain open here, as well
as its relationship to Psalms 89 and 132.

26 IQSa 2:11ff. and 2:17ff.; IQM 5:1 as compared with
15:4-6, etc. The mutilated texts 4QPB 4f. and 4QpIs[a] fragment
D are perhaps similar.

27 Material in Strack-Billerbeck, Kommentar, IV, 462ff.,
789ff.; Ginzberg, op. cit., 340ff.

28 IQSa 2:12-14, 19f.; IQSb 2:24 - 3:21; IQM 2:1ff.; 10:1 -
12:15; 15:4-6; 16:3-17:9; 18:5ff.; 19:11ff.

29 Numerous examples in IQHab and the other commentaries,
e.g. on Hab. 1:4, 13; 2:2, 4, 8, 15; Ps. 37:23, 32; also on
Num. 21:18 and Isa. 54:6 in CD vi, 3-8. The analogy with the
christological exegesis of early Christianity is obvious.

30 Cf. J. Carmignac, "Le retour du Docteur de Justice a la
fin des jours?" RQ I (1958/59), 235-248; G. Jeremias, op. cit.,
275ff.

31 "The Priest," eschatological: IQSa 2:19; IQM 10:2 (Deut.
20:2); possibly IQ22 4:8; IQ29 5:2. Historical: IQpHab 2:8;
4QpPs 37 2:15.
"Interpreter of Torah," eschatological: 4QFl 1:11; possibly
4QPB 5. Historical: CD vi, 7.   Uncertain: CD vii, 18.
"Teacher of Righteousness," historical: IQbHab 1:13, etc.;
cf. CD i, 11; xx, 32; eschatological: CD vi, 11.

32 This becomes especially clear if we may attribute the
Hodayoth to the Teacher - whether in part or in their entirety
is in this respect a matter of indifference.

33 G. Jeremias (op. cit., 283ff.) has demonstrated this with
respect to the Teacher of Righteousness but has failed to draw

the full consequences.

34   Thus e.g. van der Woude, op. cit., 186f.; rightly criticized by G. Jeremias, op. cit., 296ff.

35   Cf. D. Flusser, "Two Notes on the Midrash on II Sam. 7,"
IEJ 9 (1959), 99-109. According to 4QF1 1:11, the Branch of
David will appear at the end of days with the Interpreter of
the Law. But it is highly questionable that the testimony
collection was composed before the death of the interpreter of
the law/teacher of righteousness.

36   The interpretation of CD vii, 18-21 is controversial.
In the interpretation of Num. 24:17, "scepter" is related to
the "Prince of the Community" and "star" to the "Interpreter
of the Law." This seems to reflect a doctrine of two anointed
ones. But in what precedes, Amos 5:26f. is related to the
early history of the sect. Thus the question is whether the
sentence "And the star is the Interpreter of the Law coming to
Damascus" refers to the future or to the past. Both are possible grammatically. But a reference to the past is supported
both by the context and by CD vi, 7, where "Interpreter of the
Law" clearly designates the historical teacher. These difficulties are most easily resolved by the hypothesis that CD vii,
10ff. draws upon traditional testimonies which go back to a
time when the community still hoped that its teacher would become the high priest of the messianic age.

37 . Cf. M. Smith, "What is implied by the Variety of Messianic Figures?," JBL 78 (1959), 66-72.

38   Milik, op. cit., 125, note 3. A plausible explanation
of the textual data is given by J. F. Priest, "Mebaqqer, Paqid,
and the Messiah," JBL 81 (1962), 55-61.

39   CD iii, 21 - iv, 4. But elsewhere the distinction between priests, Levites and laymen is maintained (CD x, 5f.;
xiv 3ff.).

40   Cf. CD vi, 7-11; xix, 35 - xx, 1. CD vii, 18-21 must
also be interpreted in conformity with these texts. Cf. note
36 above. By assuming a reinterpretation of older traditions,
we can explain the apparently complicated teaching of the
Damascus Document fairly simply: Only one Messiah is expected
who will function as teacher (vi, 10f.; xii, 23), as ruler
(vii, 20f.; xix, 10ff.) and--probably--as priest (xiv, 19).
"Aaron and Israel" would then no longer mean priesthood and
laity, but rather the priestly-Israelite community of the new
covenant. Cf. F. F. Hvidberg, Menigheden af den nye Pagt i
Damascus (Copenhagen: Gad, 1928), 280f.

41   Cf. esp. 1 Macc. 14:4-15.

42   1 Macc. 2:26, 54. Cf. W. R. Farmer, Maccabees, Zealots,

and Josephus (New York: Columbia University Press, 1956), 178f.; and M. Hengel, Die Zeloten (Leiden: Brill, 1961), 168ff.

43 Cf. e.g. R. Meyer, Der Prophet aus Galiläa, 76-82.

44 Bell. vi, 312f.; cf. iii, 351-54, 400-402. J. Blenkin-sopp, "The Oracle of Judah and the Messianic Entry," JBL 80 (1961), 55-64.

45 Major Trends in Jewish Mysticism (3rd rev. ed.; New York: Schocken Books, 1961), 307-310.

46 Cf. A. Strobel, Untersuchungen zum eschatologischen Verzögerungsproblem (NovTSup 2; Leiden: Brill, 1961). J. Becker, Das Heil Gottes. (Göttingen: Vandenhoeck und Ruprecht, 1964).

47 Cf. my essay "The Crucified Messiah," in this volume. F. Hahn (The Titles of Jesus in Christology tr. H. Knight and G. Ogg; London: Lutterworth Press, 1969 , 172-189) comes to a somewhat similar conclusion.

48 I would support this statement even if the story of the empty tomb were purely legendary. I doubt that it is, however, with Hans von Campenhausen, cf. above p. 76 and footnote 32 to p. 36.

49 Cf. Stendahl, op. cit., 13ff.

50 This text may be understood as an interpretive paraphrase of Gen. 49:10 (Heb): "Until he (the seed) comes, to whom (the promise belongs)." Similar interpretive paraphrastic quota-tions are found, e.g., in Rom. 3:20 and 1 Cor. 15:45. The use of the designation "offspring" for the Messiah in Gal. 3:16, 19 (cf. Gen. 13:15, etc.) is analogous to (and probably derived from) the messianic interpretation of "offspring" in 2 Sam. 7:12; cf. 4QFl 1:10-12, 4QPB 4. The messianic interpretation of Gen. 3:15 (cf. 4:25 and 19:34) would also be a possible analogy if it is pre-Christian (cf. Bill., I, 958, note 1; 26f.).

51 For the outlook in the Similitudes of Enoch, cf. E. Sjöberg, Der Menschensohn im äthiopischen Henochbuch (Lund: Gleerup, 1946), 61ff.; P. L. Schoonheim, Een semasiologisch Onderzoek van Parousia (Aalten: de Boer, 1953).

52 In recent German scholarship this is done often and much too uncritically. Cf. e.g. E. Grässer, Das Problem der Parousieverzögerung (BZNW 22; Berlin: Töpelmann, 1957). F. Hahn (op. cit., 161-168; 284f.) also uncritically regards statements concerning the parousia as belonging to the oldest stratum of tradition and finds evidence for this even in Revelation and in the Lukan birth stories. English scholars

have at least seen that the emergence of Christian expectation of the parousia poses a historical problem. Cf. T. F. Glasson, The Second Advent (London: Epworth, 1945) and J. A. T. Robinson, Jesus and His Coming (London: SCM, 1957).

53 In his book Jesus and the Word (tr. L. Pettibone Smith; New York: Scribner's, 1934), Bultmann wrote: "The Message of Jesus is an eschatological gospel -- the proclamation that now the fulfillment of the promise is at hand, that now the Kingdom of God begins" (28). When in his later work Bultmann employs categories drawn from existential philosophy, this emphasis recedes in favor of a one-sided concentration on the end of the world and of history.

54 This has to be emphasized against the tendency, common since Lohmeyer, to describe Christology by means of the individual christological titles. The tendency is to view each title as the bearer of a unique christological conception and even to distinguish a "paidology" or a "kyriology" or a "hyiology" from "Christology" proper. Cf. O. Cullmann, The Christology of the New Testament (tr. F. Filson; Philadelphia: Westminster, 1964); W. Kramer, Christ, Lord, Son of God (tr. B. Hardy; Naperville: Allenson, 1966). On the basis of extant writings and Jewish analogies, we must rather assume that the conceptions were from the beginning very complex; they were shaped more by events and texts than by fixed concepts and pre-existent ideologies.

55 What G. von Rad has shown for the OT in his Old Testament Theology is even more true of post-biblical Judaism and Christianity. On this problem see R. Bultmann, "Prophecy and Fulfillment," Essays Philosophical and Theological (tr. J. C. G. Grieg; New York: Macmillan, 1955), 182-208. Cf. in addition RGG[3] VI, 1962, cols. 1584-90 and the literature there cited.

The Atonement--An Adequate Reward for the Akedah?

1 "Le sacrifice d'Isaac et la mort de Jésus." REJ 64 (1912), 161-85.

2 Paulus, Tübingen, 1959, pp. 144-52. (ET, Paul, Philadelphia, 1961, pp. 141-49). Cf. JBL 65 (1946), 385-92.

3 Jésus transfiguré, Copenhagen, 1947, pp. 86-96.

4 Jewish Symbols, New York, 1954, 4, pp. 172-94; cf. 9, pp. 71-77; 12, pp. 68-71, etc.

5 S. Spiegel, The Last Trial. Translated from the Hebrew, with an Introduction, by Judah Goldin, New York, 1967. The original essay appeared in Alexander Marx Jubilee Volume, New York, 1950.

6 Scripture and Tradition in Judaism, Leiden, 1961, pp. 193-227.

7 La nuit pascale (Analecta Biblica, 22), Rome, 1963, 133-208. "La présentation targumique du sacrifice d'Isaac et la soteriologie paulinienne." Studiorum Paulinorum Congressus Internationalis Catholicus, Rome, 1963, 2, pp. 563-74. Cf. RSR 49 (1961), 103-06. Cf. also F.-M. Braun, Jean le Théologien, 2, Les grandes traditions d'Israel, Paris, 1964, pp. 179-81, and R. A. Rosenberg, JBL 84 (1965), 374-80.

8 Cf. D. Lerch, Isaaks Opferung, christlich gedeutet, Tübingen, 1950; I. Speyart van Woerden, "The Iconography of the Sacrifice of Isaac," VC 15 (1961), 214-55; Spiegel, Last Trial, p. xi.

9 Cf. James 2:21f.; Heb. 11:17f.; cf. 6:13f.

10 Cf. Rom. 3:24f.; 4:25(?); 8:32; 1 Cor. 5:7(??); Gal. 3:13-14; Eph. 1:3+6f.(??); John 1:29; 1 Peter 1:19f.; Rev. 5:6(??).

11 Hom. 8, MPG 12, 208. Cf. Lerch and Speyart van Woerden, note 8 above.

12 E.g., Jülicher, Lietzmann, Dodd, Schlatter, Nygren, Leenhardt.

13 A Commentary on The Epistle to the Romans, London, 1956, p. 99, cf. p. 172.

14 <u>Die Schriften des Neuen Testaments</u>, 2nd ed., Göttingen, 1908, 2, p. 280.

15 On the parallelism between Rom. 5:1-11 and Rom. 8 cf. my "Two Notes on Romans 5," <u>ST</u> 5 (1951), 37-48. Today I would not argue so strongly that Rom. 1-8 should be divided in 1-4+ 5-8 rather than into 1-5+6-8. The sections 5:1-11 and 5:12-21 function both as conclusions of what precedes and as introductions to what follows.

16 Cf. e.g., R. Bultmann, <u>Theology of the New Testament</u>, New York, 1951, I, pp. 78-86, 124-33, etc. A. M. Hunter, <u>Paul and his Predecessors</u>, 2nd ed., London, 1961.

17 <u>Der Brief an die Römer</u> (Meyer, 10. ed.), Göttingen, 1955, p. 184.

18 Gen. 22:16 LXX, <u>kai</u> <u>ouk</u> <u>epheisō</u> <u>tou</u> <u>huiou</u> <u>sou</u> <u>tou</u> <u>agapētou</u>. Hebrew, w^{e}lō' hāsaktā 'et binkā 'et y^{e}hidekā.

19 <u>ta</u> <u>panta</u> is related to the cosmic outlook in Rom. 8, esp. vv. 17-23 and 35-39. For the promises to Abraham, cf. Gen. 12:7; 13:14-17; 22:17f.; 26:3-5; etc., and the interpretation implied in passages like Rom. 4:13; Gal. 3:16-18 and 4:7. Cf. esp. Zahn and Michel.

20 It may here be sufficient to mention names like Dodd, Danielou, Daube, Doeve, Stendahl, Lindars, Ellis, Vermes, Gerhardsson, and Borgen.

21 Barnabas 7:3; Melito, Paschal Homily 59 (431); 69 (499); fr. 9. Cf. J. Danielou, <u>Sacramentum futuri</u>, Paris, 1950, pp. 97-111. Vermes, <u>op. cit.</u>, p. 220, finds that "the Akedah merely prefigures the redemption by Christ," and Le Deaut, <u>Nuit Pascale</u>, p. 203, still tends to subsume all New Testament allusions to Gen. 22 under "l'aggadah typologique propre à la perpective chrétienne."

22 Not even John 3:14 would be a real analogy.

23 Adv. Haer. 4, 5, 4. A fragment of the Greek text is preserved: <u>prothymōs</u> <u>ton</u> <u>idion</u> <u>monogenē</u> <u>kai</u> <u>agapēton</u> (+ <u>huion ?</u>) <u>parachōrēsas</u> <u>thysian</u> <u>tō</u> <u>theō</u>, <u>hina</u> <u>kai</u> <u>ho</u> <u>theos</u> <u>eudokēsē</u> <u>hyper</u> <u>tou</u> <u>spermatos</u> <u>autou</u> <u>pantos</u> <u>ton</u> <u>idion</u> <u>monogenē</u> <u>kai</u> <u>agapēton</u> <u>huion</u> <u>thysian</u> <u>paraschein</u> <u>eis</u> <u>lytrōsin</u> <u>hēmeteran</u>.

24 "Qui et advocavit per fidem deum quoniam (<u>vel</u> ut) pro humanitate pro filio retribuit (<u>vel</u> retribueret) ipse." Latin translation by Mercier in <u>Irénée de Lyon, Contre les hérésies</u>, <u>livre</u> IV, ed. A. Rousseau, Paris, 1965.

25 In fact, Irenaeus seems to draw upon old traditions. Thus, Isaac is seen as a prototype for Christians who are to carry their cross, rather than as a prefiguration of Christ.

In the present context the "Word of God," whose commandment Abraham obeyed, is the pre-existent Logos, but originally it may have been God's memra. Elsewhere Irenaeus has certainly preserved interpretations of "presbyters" and even fragments of Hebrew-Christian midrash, cf. N. Brox, Offenbarung, Gnosis, und gnostischer Mythos bei Irenaus von Lyon, Salzburg/München, 1966, pp. 83, n. 103 and pp. 150-57, with literature.

26 Matt. 7:1f.; Luke 6:37f.; Mishnah Sotah 1:7-9, etc. Cf., e.g., H. Ljungman, Guds barmhärtighet och dom, Lund, 1950, pp. 25-30.

27 Cf. 4 Macc. 7:14; 13:12; 16:20. Isaac's willingness is also stressed by Josephus, Ant. I, 232, and Ps.-Philo, Ant. Bibl. 32:3; 40:2. Cf. Vermes, op. cit., pp. 197-204. This emphasis does not diminish the role of Abraham, who is a model for the mother of the seven brothers in 4 Macc.

28 Riesenfeld, Jésus transfiguré, pp. 86-96, argues to the contrary, on the basis of a very broad use of the term Messiah.

29 The evidence is conveniently summarized by Vermes, Scripture and Tradition, pp. 206-08. Of special interest is an exegesis of Ps. 79:11 (and 102:21) according to which the one in fetters ('āsîr) and close to death (tᵉmûtāh, cf. Jastrow s.v.) is Isaac, whose children God will set free. This interpretation is presupposed already by R. Joshua (ca. 100 C.E.), who makes God speak to Isaac with the words of the psalm, Mekilta de-Rabbi Simeon on Exod. 6:2 (ed. Hoffmann, p. 4). Cf. Pesikta 31 (or 32), ed. Buber, 200 b (in spite of Vermes, p. 207, n. 6).

30 Vermes, op. cit., pp. 208-14.

31 Cf. Targums Lv 22:14; Le Déaut, Nuit pascale, pp. 171f.

32 Targum Neofiti, Gen. 22:14. The other versions differ only on minor points; cf. Le Déaut, op. cit., pp. 154, 163-69.

33 j Taan 2:4, 65d, in the translation of J. Goldin, Spiegel, Last Trial, p. 90. Cf. the various texts treated by Spiegel on pp. 89-98. R. Johanan lived in the third century, but the contrast between Gen. 21:12 and Gen. 22 is already stressed in Heb. 11:18.

34 Text in e.g. The Authorized Daily Prayer Book, ed. J. H. Hertz, Rev. ed., New York, 5709/1948, p. 882. The additions in parenthesis are taken from Goldin's translation of Spiegel, op. cit., p. 89. Cf. also GnR 56:10, translated by Goldin, p. 90.

35 Spiegel, Last Trial, p. 93.

36 Gen. 22:3-Exod. 14:21. Mekilta be-Shallah 4, on Exod. 14:15 (Lauterbach, I, 218).

37 R. Haninah, fourth generation Amoraim, GnR 56:5.

38 Gen. 22:5-Exod. 24:1-Isa. 27:13. Lekah Tob, p. 98.

39 GnR 56:1. Cf. Spiegel, Last Trial, pp. 109-16, re notes 36-39.

40 ExR 15:17; 44:4.

41 Mekilta Be-Shallah I, on Exod. 13:21 (Lauterbach I, pp. 184f.). The further references are to Gen. 18:4; Num. 21:17; 18:5; Exod. 16:4; 18:7; Num. 11:13; 18:4; Ps. 105:39; 18:18; Exod. 12:23. The text as a whole is inspired by Ps. 105:39-42. For the principle of adequate retribution cf. already Wis. 11:15ff.; 15:18ff., etc.

42 Cf. Gal. 3:16 and 19; Acts 3:25f.

43 Cf. Bultmann, Theology, I, p. 46; E. Käsemann, Exegetische Versuche und Besinnungen I, Göttingen, 1960, pp. 96-100 = ZNW 43 (1950/51), 150-54; J. Reumann, Int. 10 (1966), 432-52.

44 Thus Schoeps, Paul, p. 146, following G. Klein, Studien über Paulus, Stockholm, 1918, p. 96. Cf. Le Déaut, "Présentation targumique," 571f.

45 Cf. Rom. 1:13; Eph. 1:9. This interpretation has been defended quite apart from the question of allusion to Gen. 22, cf. C. Bruston, ZNW 7 (1906), 77. Cf. also J. H. Moulton and G. Milligan, The Vocabulary of the Greek New Testament, London, [2]1915, p. 554.

46 But cf. the use of 'izdammen, yizdammen, or yibhar, in the Targums; Le Déaut, Nuit Pascale, pp. 157f. and 171.

47 Cf. Ps.-Philo, Ant. Bibl. 18:5, "Pro sanguine eius eligisti istos." See also note 29 above.

48 Thus a solution is provided for a problem felt by Reumann, Int. 20 (1966), 40-42. Is Gen. 22:18 reflected also in ho eulogēsas hēmas ... en Christō, Eph. 1:3 (cf. 1:6f.)? Cf. also the paraphrase in Ant. Bibl. 32:2, "In me adnuntiabuntur generationes."

49 Dion. Hal. 7, 37. Cf. J. M. Creed, JTS 41 (1940), 28-30, and literature referred to in note 43 above.

50 dia tēn paresin could also be taken to indicate the causa finalis, "So that the prosecution .... could be dropped." In the translation dia pisteōs has been left out as a Pauline comment. How far parts of v. 26 belonged to tradition may here remain an open question.

51 Texts given by Spiegel, Last Trial, pp. 90-92, cf. n. 33 above. Cf. already Jub 18:12, "And the prince Mastema was put

to shame." According to <u>Ant</u>. <u>Bibl</u>. 32:1, 4 the mouths of
envious angels were shut.

52   The notion of the covenant is imported into the text of
the fragment by Käsemann, <u>op</u>. <u>cit</u>., n. 43 above. Cf. P.
Stuhlmacher, <u>Gottes Gerechtigkeit bei Paulus</u>, Göttingen, 1965,
p. 89. Apart from exegetical details, however, my results
concur with Käsemann's.

53   Cf. <u>eis</u> <u>to</u> <u>einai</u> <u>auton</u> <u>dikaion</u> Rom. 3:26; cf. Isa. 45:21,
Neh. 9:8; H. Ljungman, <u>Pistis</u>, Lund, 1964, pp. 37, 106, etc.

54   Vermes, <u>Scripture and Tradition</u>, pp. 221f., has seen that
the Akedah motif was not introduced by Paul, but has not attempted to distinguish between Paul's interpretation and the
inherited materials with which he worked.

55   This would also apply to passages like Rom. 4:25; 5:5-10;
1 Cor. 5:7; Eph. 1:7; and Col. 1:13f. The question whether or
not they contain any allusion may therefore be left open.

56   Rom. 3:27 (cf. 2:17ff.); 4:1-5.

57   Rom. 4:4.

58   Cf. esp. Rom. 4:17, Abraham believed in God, "who makes
the dead alive." In Jewish tradition the second of the
Eighteen Benedictions ("Who makes the dead alive") was connected with the Akedah. Spiegel, <u>Last Trial</u>, 28-37. Cf.
already Heb. 11:19 and 4 Mac. 7:19; 13:17; 15:3; 16:25.

59   Rom. 2:23, cf. vv. 29-30; 10:12; and also Gal. 2:14b and
the possible addition of <u>pantōn</u> in Rom. 8:32.

60   Rom. 1:16; 3:2; 9:4f.

61   Rom. 11:28.

62   Rom. 15:8f. The phrase <u>hyper</u> <u>alētheias</u> <u>theou</u> is virtual-
ly synonymous with <u>eis</u> <u>endeiksin</u> <u>tēs</u> <u>dikaiosynēs</u> <u>autou</u>, as
shown by 3:3-7.

63   Cf., e.g., J. Munck, <u>Paul and the Salvation of Mankind</u>,
Richmond, 1959, pp. 255-81; J. Jeremias, <u>Jesus' Promise to the
Nations</u>, London and Naperville, 1958, pp. 55-73.

64   Rom. 8:32; John 3:16. The phrase, "God sent his Son,"
might be a variation of this; cf. esp. Gal. 4:3f. Influence
from Wisdom terminology is assumed by E. Schweizer, <u>ZNW</u> 57
(1966), 194-210; <u>TDNT</u> 8, pp. 376f.

65   Cf. also "My beloved Son," Mark 1:11, etc. Cf., e.g.,
Vermes, <u>Scripture and Tradition</u>, pp. 221-25. Due to the
possibility of various connotations and biblical allusions it
is hard to know the extent to which the New Testament use of

terms like <u>monogenēs</u>, <u>huios</u> <u>agapētos</u>, and <u>amnos</u> was originally derived from Gen. 22. There is only scant evidence for the theory of Vermes, pp. 202f., that Isa. 53 was related to the Akedah in pre-Christian Judaism.

66 The fact that early traditions associate the Akedah with Passover, rather than with New Year, should be mentioned here. Cf. Spiegel, Vermes, and Le Deaut.

67 Spiegel, <u>Last Trial</u>, pp. 81-86, 103f., 113, etc., thinks that ancient pagan beliefs, suppressed in Judaism, continued and returned in Christianity from Paul onward.

68 Spiegel, <u>Last Trial</u>, p. xvi.

Postscript

1 My translation. Cf. Dinkler's essay, "Petrusbekkenntnis und Satanwort," in Zeit und Geschichte (Tübingen: Mohr, 1964).

2 Hahn, The Titles of Jesus, p. 160f. It may here be added that Mark never says that the inscription was nailed to the cross, in contrast to Matt. 27:37 and John 19:19. As there is no evidence that a titulus was nailed to the cross, one should better speak of the "inscription of the charge."

3 "Christologie und neutestamentliche Chronologie," in H. Baltensweiler und Bo Reicke, ed. Neues Testament und Geschichte (Festschrift O. Cullmann, Zürich: Theologischer Verlag, Tübingen: Mohr, 1972), p. 53. Hengel here refers to an extensive footnote in Hahn's Christologische Hoheitstitel (Göttingen: Vandenhoeck & Ruprecht, 1963), p. 212, 3, which has been left out in the English translation.

4 NTS 8 (1961-62), 101-116. Quotation from p. 115.

5 What Do We Know About Jesus? (Philadelphia: Westminster, 1968), p. 86. Cf. "Die Frage nach dem messianischen Bewusstsein Jesu," Nov T 6 (1963), 20-48.

6 The Messiah and the Temple, Unpublished dissertation, Yale 1973.

7 NTS 15 (1968-69), 153-167.

8 "Var det noe alternativ til Messias?" SEA, 37-38 (1972-73), 21-34.

9 It may here be sufficient to refer to James M. Robinson, Helmut Koester, Trajectories through Early Christianity (Philadelphia: Fortress, 1971), esp. pp. 71ff. and 158ff.